TOUCHING THE HEART OF GOD

TOUCHING THE HEART OF GOD

THROUGH CREATIVE INTERCESSION

By Elizabeth Hanson Aguilar

XULON PRESS

Xulon Press
2301 Lucien Way #415
Maitland, FL 32751
407.339.4217
www.xulonpress.com

ISBN-13: 978-1-6322-1429-4

Dedicated to those who moved me most to discover what creative intercession is all about...

To my dear mother, Grace,
who spent her life demonstrating her name,

To my charming brother, Rolly,
who will always be my hero,

To my precious daughter, Kirsten,
who has given me Earth's greatest joy and treasures,

To my four treasured grandchildren:
Kaleb, Katrina, Jaydon, and Jennica,
who bring sunlight through the clouds, and

To my Advocate Jesus,
who paid the price I could not pay.

About the Author

*E*lizabeth Hanson Aguilar lived most of her life in the State of Washington, spent a few years in Ohio, and now resides in Austin, Texas. For over thirty years, she was a language teacher in both private and public schools, on both elementary and high school levels. She also worked at the headquarters of Aglow International for ten years, where she was able to use her Spanish and travel throughout Latin America. While working in that office, she was blessed to author the local handbook that was used by women leaders in many countries where the ministry of Aglow was established.

Now in her retirement years, she is enjoying time with family and writing Christian materials with the hope that they will encourage her family, friends, and others who are growing in their faith. Her greatest desire is to see the Kingdom of God established on the Earth and for the body of Christ to bring glory to Jesus.

Table of Contents

Introduction

"*Y*ou wonder what you are," said Chuck Pierce, a well known and highly respected present-day prophet of the Lord, who then continued, "You are an intercessor." Never will I forget those words or what they meant to me as I was considering a career change at the time. They met my soul with an odd combination of relief and disbelief. "Who, me?" was my immediate inward response. "I'm a teacher. Yeah right," continued my inner dialogue. "Sure I feel called to prayer, but I'm not like the other intercessors who spend hours on their knees or who wake up in the middle of the night and intercede so obediently. Maybe that's what I'm supposed to be doing…" and so continued the thoughts, the doubts…not just during that night's meeting, but for many years to come. But these prophetic words became part of my soul, interwoven into all my spiritual thoughts and actions. They seemed to become a lighthouse that would shine through times of dense fog and stormy seas. They never left my heart although for many years I wondered what it really meant to be an intercessor.

Of course, right away I read many books on the subject and listened to many teachings. I felt inspired hearing the stories of the great intercessors, but all the while I wondered if I were failing in my calling because I didn't have similar stories of miraculous results of God-led intercession. I just never seemed to measure up (in my mind) to those other intercessors. I would at times try to be more like them, to spend longer hours alone with the Lord, to pray more in the Spirit, all the things I felt I might be lacking, until finally I began to ask the Lord what that meant. Or perhaps I never outwardly asked the question, but the gentle Holy Spirit just began to reveal to me what those words were to mean to my life. And the answer to that question, which has been coming in pieces over recent decades, is the subject of this study.

I call this study *Touching the Heart of God* because my greatest desire is to please God and to grow in my understanding of what breaks His heart and what brings Him great delight. I want my prayers to touch God's heart. My subtitle is about *Creative Intercession* because our Creator has many, many creative ways to accomplish His purposes on the Earth, and I believe each life in God's hands can actually be a form of intercession. This happens as we learn to bring all that we touch in the natural or earthly realm into the Kingdom of God. My role as an intercessor is simply to partner with God by knowing His heart and to bring my concerns to Him, trusting that intercession is indeed happening through my life.

During this study I will share scenes and lessons that have brought me closer to the heart of God over the years, as well as key Scriptures that are life changing. My prayer for you is that you will take to heart and meditate on all the verses mentioned (from the Amplified Bible) and see how they apply to your life. And *"in a humble (gentle, modest) spirit receive and welcome the Word which implanted and rooted (in your hearts) contains the power to save your souls." James 1:21b*

Chapter 1:
The Great Intercessor, Priest and King

"Entering the Royal Priesthood"

Praying or interceding...

When I first heard I was to be an intercessor, I was unclear what that actually meant. "How is intercession that different from praying?" I wondered. "Is it just more hours on my knees, more tears and more anguish?" Scenes of impassioned intercession came to my mind. "Intercessors can be pretty weird," I thought, "and can do some strange things." To be honest, I wasn't sure I *could* do that or even that I *wanted* to.

1. What do you think intercession means?

   _____

   _____

   Are you called to be an intercessor? If so, explain how and when you knew this.

   _____

   _____

   Do you have any doubts or concerns about what it means to be an intercessor?

   _____

   _____

I decided to put the word "intercessor" on a shelf in my mind for a time while I learned more about what it meant. Fortunately I knew, at that time, some highly respected intercessors, and so I learned from them. I paid attention to their lives and prayers, and even prayed alongside them at times. My prayers didn't seem much different from theirs, I noticed, although these intercessors did seem very closely in tune with God. They didn't over-explain things to God in their prayers; they probably knew He already understood what they were saying. They prayed with an odd blend of *humility* and *authority*. To sum it up, they spoke to God <u>as if they actually knew what was on His mind and in His heart</u>.

At this point in time, I began to catch glimpses of what intercession seemed to be about. I also read books and listened to speakers as they shared some of the marvelous things God did through their intercession. I began to wonder if intercession was a special calling on the lives of just a chosen group of believers, <u>or if *all Christians* are actually intercessors</u>. Some people certainly seemed to act more like intercessors, but again, was it just that they prayed more?

2. How do you think intercessory prayer is different from other prayers? Do you think all Christians intercede in some way?

_____

_____

Do you personally know any intercessors that you have learned from? _____

If so, who are they and what are some main things you have learned from them?

_____

_____

One dictionary definition of *pray* is "to make a reverent petition to a deity" but *intercede* goes beyond this to mean "<u>to make an entreaty in favor of another, to mediate, or act as an intermediary, especially to seek to resolve differences between two or more conflicting parties, to be in the middle</u>." I began to conclude that since my prayers usually were on behalf of other people, they could be called intercessory prayers. Maybe I really was an intercessor!

3. Think back to significant times of prayer you've had. How often were you praying for others rather than yourself? Give an example or two.

_____

_____

_____

_____

Sometimes it is only in looking back over our lives that we see our questions have been answered. Now, many years after I first considered myself to be an intercessor, I finally am exploring and recording the thoughts and questions on this subject that lay beneath the surface of my entire life. In retrospect, I see now that my whole Christian life has been one of intercession.

> **My hope in writing this study is that you too will see how intercession has been a part of your Christian life, and that you will understand how it connects you to the Father's heart and helps bring His Kingdom to the Earth. Your intercession is a unique as you are!**

So to begin, we will look at the One Person who can answer all the questions we might have about this subject. We turn our eyes onto Jesus, the Source and Finisher of our faith *"Who is at the right hand of God actually pleading as He intercedes for us" Romans 8:34b*

Jesus alone could meet the need...

Ever since the Great Mistake made by Adam and Eve, mankind has been separated from the Creator, from the Father. <u>No amount of man's effort or sacrifice could bridge the gap made by sin, until the cross</u>. When God's only Son gave up His life on the cross, the only acceptable sacrifice was made. The cross of Jesus was the act of intervention that still stands between sinful man and a holy God. Like Jesus Himself said, *"No one comes to the Father except through Me." (John 14:6)* Consider all the sufferings Job endured and how he longed to have a mediator bridge the gap between him and God. *Job 16:21 "<u>Oh, that there were one who might plead for a man with God</u> and that he might maintain his right with Him, as a son of man pleads with or for his neighbor!"* And praise God, He sent His Son to be just that.

I remember reading a passage in *Isaiah* and thinking that God wants people who would also stand in the gap to bring His will to the earth. This is the role of the intercessor, but I think it's essential to focus on the end of the passage. *"And the Lord saw it, and it displeased Him that there was no justice. And He saw that there was no man and wondered that <u>there was no intercessor</u> (no one to intervene on behalf of truth and right); <u>therefore</u> His own arm brought Him victory, and His own righteousness (having the Spirit without measure) sustained him." (Isaiah 56:15b-16)* It was God's own arm that brought Him victory. It was God's very own Son that was raised up to intercede for a lost world.

I love how Paul opened his letter to the Galatians with a blessing and strong reminder: *"Grace and spiritual blessing be to you and soul peace from God the Father and our <u>Lord Jesus Christ (the Messiah) Who gave (yielded) Himself up to atone for our sins and to save and sanctify us,</u> in order to rescue and <u>deliver us from the present wicked age and world order,</u> in accordance with the will and purpose and plan of our God and Father—To Him be ascribed all the glory through all the ages of the ages and the eternities of the eternities! Amen (so be it). Galatians 1:3-5* Paul often preached a whole sermon in his greeting. He never hesitated to remind believers what the Christian life was really about, the gift of Christ Himself.

As we live our lives, we are called to partner with the Holy Spirit to fulfill God's plan and purposes on the Earth. However, the power behind our intercession is not because of our efforts; it is always because of the victory of Jesus Christ. Although we may be immensely grateful for God's intercessors in the world today, it's important that we always remember that it is only Jesus who was able to intervene on behalf of mankind. It is only His cross that can bridge the gap between the lost world and the Kingdom of God. The work was completed with His words on the cross: *"It is finished." (John 19:30)* At that moment the debt was paid in full. The call to intercede is simply the call to become one with God, to remain tightly connected to Him, and then to speak out what is on His heart as we carry out the lives He has purposed for each of us.

4. Can you think of a time when you were interceding for a person or situation when the burden became too great? Was the Lord reminding you that He had already paid the price and won the victory?

The importance of Jesus' blood...

Before I go further into intercession and how we are able to intercede for others, I want to focus on the blood Christ shed on the cross. *"But you were purchased with the precious blood of Christ (the Messiah), like that of a sacrificial lamb without blemish or spot." I Peter 1:19.* It was Jesus' blood that brought us into the kingdom of God.

I John 1:7 explains *"But if we really are living and walking in the Light, as He Himself is in the Light, we have true, unbroken fellowship with one another, and the blood of Jesus Christ His Son cleanses (removes) us from all sin and guilt (keeps us cleansed from sin in all its forms and manifestations).* So let's focus on the significance of Christ's blood a bit more.

You probably already know how ancient civilizations always focused on blood sacrifices. I think of the brutal sacrifices the Aztecs made on top of the ancient pyramids that still stand in Mexico as a reminder of the roots of that country. The sacrifice of the most innocent, the babies, was obviously inspired by Satan himself. The ancient religions, like Baal worship, that we read about in the Old Testament also focused on blood and infant sacrifices. The purpose of this study is not to explore this subject in depth but rather to pose the question: Why were all these ancient cultures and satanic groups so focused on blood sacrifices? <u>The devil obviously recognizes there is a special significance in blood sacrifice. Why</u>?

<u>Life is in the blood</u>. Think about your own blood a minute and what it means to your body, your health, your very life. It's <u>the circulation of blood that enables</u> all your bodily organs to function. Without it, there can be no life. Why did God create our bodies to work like that? We as Christians are sometimes referred to as the <u>body</u> of Christ. Can we then conclude how we as His body need the circulation of His blood in order to function as we should? I titled this study *Touching the Heart of God*, and it's interesting to remember the connection between physical hearts and the blood that pumps through them. How then can we, as Christ's body, function unless God's people begin to recognize the role that Christ's blood must play in our daily lives? I believe we are beginning to gain greater revelation about this because it has been almost overlooked in recent years.

5. Comment on the significance of human blood in sacrifices or in daily bodily function.

_____

_____

_____

_____

_____

You may be aware that God instructed His people quite clearly how to sacrifice in Leviticus and throughout the Old Testament. Have you ever pondered why God was so exact that the <u>sacrifice had to be perfect</u>? Hopefully you are well aware of how Jesus became the spotless Lamb that was to fulfill all the laws governing sacrifice. That's the heart of the New Testament.

Have you ever wondered why God was not pleased with Cain's sacrifice (the fruits of his labor in the fields) but was well pleased with Abel's sacrifice (the firstborn of his sheep)? (See ***Genesis chapter 4.***) After Cain killed his brother in jealous anger, the Lord said to him, "What have you done? The voice of <u>your brother's blood is crying to Me from the ground</u>.*"(Genesis 4:10)* And from then on the land was cursed and no longer able to yield its strength because it had opened its mouth to receive Abel's shed blood (See ***Genesis 4:11-12*.**) This makes me think of how the blood of those martyred for God is crying out for justice, but that's a whole study in itself. The writer of Hebrews explains more: ***"And to Jesus, the Mediator (Go-between, <u>Agent</u>) of a new covenant, and <u>to the sprinkled</u>***

blood which speaks of mercy), a better and nobler and more gracious message than the blood of Abel (which cried out for vengeance)." Hebrews 12:24

My point here is to draw your attention to the role that blood has played since God first created the world. God knows the value of the blood; angels, demons, and all powers and principalities know the value. But do God's people? Why is it so rare to hear preachers speak on the power of Christ's blood? I believe Christ's blood is Satan's greatest dread; how he hates and probably cowers and flees when he hears that mentioned.

Yet many churches today only mention the power of Christ's blood in passing, perhaps at Easter and as they perform their communion services. If it really is our very life, shouldn't it be emphasized often? To show that taking communion is extremely important; Jesus told His disciples to do this often in remembrance of Him. (See *Luke 22:17-20*.) The work of the cross, the breaking of Jesus' body and the spilling of His precious blood, must be the crux of our Christian faith and the power behind all our prayers for it is the basis of the New Covenant that we as Christians enjoy.

One day many years ago I heard the Holy Spirit speak to my heart that I would come to know that *Jesus' blood is enough...enough for everything.* I'm still growing in my understanding of this truth, but I hope to remind us here to apply Christ's blood more often or to plead His blood (an old fashioned and much needed practice today) over every person, place or situation as we pray. Without recognizing and applying Christ's blood, our prayers may simply become petitions or even empty words. God wants to remind us of the price Jesus paid to redeem anything and everybody and to show us how to pray with this understanding and authority. May we all come humbly to the Father as Jesus' disciples did when they said, ***"Lord, teach us to pray." Luke 11:1.***

6. Write out a simple prayer asking God to cover a person or situation with the blood of Jesus; then speak it out loud.

_____

_____

_____

_____

_____

_____

I remember while I worked at the headquarters of Aglow International, I was upset one day because I heard a colleague of mine lie about me. As it really bothered me, I went to the head of our Human Resource Department, Elaine, and told her. I thought she would empathize with my plight and maybe even bring that colleague in for a "talk," but instead she replied, "<u>You need to put this under the blood of Jesus</u>." My mind, of course, thought that sounded like a Christian cliché, but because I respected and trusted Elaine's judgment, I did just that. I said out loud, "Lord I commit this person to You, and put this offense under the blood of Jesus." To my grateful amazement, from that moment on it never bothered me again, and I remained good friends with my sister. Oh, how the Lord would have <u>everyone of His children deal with offenses this way</u>. Isn't it time for His body to quit falling for Satan's bait, judging all who offend us or that we disagree with? May we all learn how to surrender ourselves, our own opinions, and to apply the precious blood of Jesus to our daily interactions and our prayers.

7. Have you ever responded to an offense by putting it all under Christ's blood? If so, explain. If not, why not write out a simple prayer asking God to cover a person or situation with the blood of Jesus; then speak it out loud.

_____

_____

_____

_____

A royal priesthood...

Perhaps you know all about a priest's duties. They actually are called to teach, baptize, and intercede for the people by offering sacrifices to God for their sins in the Holy of Holies. Studying the ancient priests is interesting; but for now, let me just say that our focus is on Jesus as High Priest. In the wonderful book of Hebrews, we learn more about Jesus in this role. ***"Inasmuch then as <u>we have a great High Priest</u> Who has (already) ascended and passed through the heavens, Jesus the son of God, let us <u>hold fast our confession (of faith in Him)</u>. For we do not have a High Priest Who is unable to understand and sympathize and have a shared feeling with our weaknesses and infirmities and liability to the assaults of temptation, but One Who has been tempted in every respect as we are; yet without sinning." Hebrews 4:14-15*** That's why we are encouraged to confidently bring all that we are interceding for before His throne of grace ***"that we may receive <u>mercy (for our failures) and find grace to help</u> in good time for every need (appropriate help and well-timed help, coming just when we need it)." (Verse 16)***

TOUCHING THE HEART OF GOD

All the way through the Old Testament there was a clear <u>distinction between the role of the priest</u> <u>and that of the king</u>. In fact, you may recall in *I Samuel 13: 8-14* that <u>King Saul lost his royal</u> <u>anointing</u> because he impatiently went into the temple and offered the sacrifice that only the priest was allowed to bring. The Prophet Samuel rebuked him by saying*, "You have done foolishly! You have not kept the commandment of the Lord your God which He commanded you; for the Lord would have established your kingdom over Israel forever; but now your kingdom shall not continue; the Lord has sought out (David) a man after His own heart..."(verses 13-14)*

However, Jesus not only was the Great High Priest but also the King of Kings. *"And from Jesus Christ the faithful and trustworthy Witness, the First-born of the dead (first to be brought back to life) and the Prince (Ruler) of the kings of the earth. To Him Who ever loves us and has once (for all) loosed and <u>freed us from our sins by His own blood, and formed us into a kingdom (a royal race), priests</u> to His God and Father—to Him be the glory and the power."* *Revelation 1:5-6* This verse in Revelation refers to end times: *"They will wage war against the Lamb, and <u>the Lamb will triumph over them; for He is Lord of lords and King of kings</u>— and those with Him and on His side are chosen and called (elected) and loyal and faithful followers." Revelation 17:14* <u>What an awesome privilege we have to be His royal and priestly</u> <u>followers.</u>

Our role, then, as intercessors joined to Jesus, is to live wherever we are with His heart of sacrifice and surrender but also with His kingdom authority. We are to come boldly before the throne of grace as a priest would present a sacrifice, <u>knowing that the Lamb of God was the perfect sac-</u> <u>rifice</u>. We are to <u>lift the person up to God and surrender all our thoughts and wishes for how God</u> <u>will intervene in this situation</u>. That is our role as a priest. But then we are <u>to move into our royal</u> <u>role and make decrees or confessions of faith</u> that line up with the Word Himself.

As God's intercessors, <u>we are to act as a royal priesthood</u>. We are allowed to regularly enter the Holy of Holies, and here is a passage that we would benefit remembering. *"Therefore, brethren, since <u>we have full freedom and confidence</u> to enter into the Holy of Holies (by the power and virtue in the blood of Jesus, by this fresh (new) and living way which <u>He initiated and ded-</u> <u>icated and opened for us</u> through the separating curtain (veil of the Holy of Holies), that is through His flesh, and since we have such a great and wonderful and noble Priest (Who rules) over the house of God, <u>let us all come forward and draw near with true (honest and sincere)</u> <u>hearts in unqualified assurance and absolute conviction</u> engendered by faith (by that leaning of the entire human personality on God <u>in absolute trust and confidence in His power, wisdom,</u> <u>and goodness,</u> having our hearts sprinkled and purified from a guilty (evil) conscience and our bodies cleansed with pure water." Hebrews 10:19-22*

Peter explains the role of an intercessor this way. *"But you are a <u>chosen race, a royal priesthood,</u> a dedicated nation (God's) own purchased, special people, that you may set forth the wonderful deeds and display the virtues and perfection of Him Who called you out of darkness* *into His marvelous light." I Peter 2:9* <u>We are to fulfill the role of a priest in our prayers but also to move in kingly authority</u>. Let us not forget that as a royal priesthood, we connect both with the Lamb and with the King. I know the lion and the lamb lying down together in heaven is a symbol of Peace, but might that suggest we are to live in peace as we live as a royal priesthood?

8. Think of a person or situation that is now separated from God's will or purposes . How might you intercede as a priest before God's throne of grace?

_____

_____

_____

_____

_____

_____

Praying with authority...

So in discussing our <u>role in God's royal priesthood, let's remember that in addition to our humble role as priests, we are given a powerful role of authority</u>. Once we have surrendered our burden by touching God's heart, we begin to discover what His will is. We then join our hearts and our words to those of the King of kings. Remember a king reigns, rules, utters edicts, begins and ends battles and such. <u>His words have absolute authority, and even he cannot take back what he has declared.</u> Remember the position King Xerxes faced in the book of Esther after he learned of Haman's deception and desire to destroy the Jews? He could not undo his edict but was able to add another edict giving the Jews the right to defend themselves*. (See Esther 8-9.)* So when God promises you something, you can be assured that <u>He will not change His mind. His Word will never return to Him void, *(See Isaiah 55:1.)*</u>

As we intercede, the Lord would tell us, *"So get rid of all uncleanness and the rampant outgrowth of wickedness, and in a humble (gentle, modest) spirit receive and <u>welcome the Word which contains the power to save your souls.</u>" James 1:21.* Then once we receive that word or promise, we are to hold onto it and make it our confession of faith. We may have no idea how our confession changes the spiritual realm. *Ephesians 3:10* says: *(The purpose is) that <u>through the church the complicated, many-sided wisdom of God</u> in all its infinite variety and innumerable aspects <u>might now be made known to the angelic rulers and authorities (principalities and powers) in the heavenly sphere,</u>"* <u>Never underestimate the power of your prayer when it is in tune with the heart of God.</u>

Job 22:21-30 begins: *"Acquaint now yourself with Him (agree with God and show yourself to be conformed to His will) and be at peace; by that (you shall prosper and great) good shall come to you. Receive, I pray you, the law and instruction from His mouth and lay up His words in your heart..."* And the passage concludes with, *"<u>You shall also decide and decree a thing, and it shall be established for you</u>; and the light (of God's favor) shall shine upon your ways. When they make you low, you will say, There is a lifting up; and the humble person He lifts up and saves. He will even deliver the one (for whom you intercede) who is not innocent; yes, he will be delivered through the cleanness of your hands."* What confidence that should give us as we pray and intercede.

9. Think about the authority of King Jesus and how you agree with Him. Then record what you think God is saying about how to intercede and what the results will be.

_____

_____

_____

_____

_____

_____

The gift of God's wisdom...

<u>The heart of a priest in God's Kingdom, is humble and willing to surrender all, to sacrifice one's own perspective to the higher ways of Almighty God.</u> We do well to remember these words in ***Isaiah chapter 55, verses 8-9 : "For <u>my thoughts are not your thoughts</u>, neither are your ways My ways, says the Lord. For as the heavens are higher than the earth, so are My ways higher than your ways and My thoughts than your thoughts."*** As we pray, it is always good to join our words to our Savior's who said (as He was about to pay the ultimate sacrifice of His life), ***"Father, if You are willing, remove this cup from Me; <u>yet not My will, but (always) yours be done</u>." (Luke 22:42)*** I can't help but wonder if sometimes the answers to our prayers are delayed because God is waiting for us to give up our own ideas of how things should be worked out, surrendering to and trusting in His perfect will.

As intercessors, we must always seek to touch God's heart with our needs and to be willing to have Him change our heart and mind. For over twenty years, I interceded for my daughter's marriage to be a better reflection of God's purposes. After years of turmoil and stress, nothing ever got better.

Finally as their marriage seemed to be ending, I felt the Lord's release me from this intercession when I heard the question, "What do you think is more important: that this marriage continue or that your daughter fulfill the destiny I have for her life?" <u>My perspective had to change</u>. Now please do not misunderstand what I am saying; God spoke to our hearts in many ways to know this was His will. We cannot make a rule or formula about what God's will is based on one situation for our God is much bigger than this and will not be put in a "box" of our own understanding. <u>We must each seek God's heart about our intercession and ask Him clearly to give us His wisdom</u>. ***"If any of you is deficient in wisdom, let him ask of the giving God** (Who gives) **to everyone liberally and ungrudgingly, without reproaching or faultfinding, and it will be given him. Only <u>it must be in faith</u> that he ask with no wavering (no hesitating, no doubting)." James 1:5-6.*

10. Has there ever been a time when you have interceded a long time for a person and finally come to the conclusion that <u>God may have different ideas about how the situation is best resolved</u>? Or perhaps that thought is just occurring to you now. Remember, it's always <u>hard to give up our way of thinking about how things should be worked out</u>, but coming to that <u>point of surrender may bring the breakthrough you are hoping for</u>. What idea or way of thinking do you feel God might want you to surrender to His perfect will?

_____

_____

_____

_____

The heart issue of trust...

Believing is an act of the will, beginning in the mind, but as it progresses more deeply to the heart, it becomes a heart issue. We may seek wisdom and come to believe a promise of God, but it is in <u>times of deep testing that our belief turns into trust</u>. As he suffered, Job declared, ***"Though He slay me, yet will I trust Him." Job 13:15***

Recently my single daughter found herself in another very difficult situation. She had relocated to another state with her work less than a year after her divorce. She had just bought a big house to provide room for herself and three of her children when she suddenly lost her job and her only source of income. Needless to say this was a scary time, as she watched the only savings she had dwindle down month after month even with her unemployment benefits. Several jobs looked promising, so we prayed and believed they would be God's provision. However, door after door soon closed. The disappointments were devastating, but the truths she learned during her seven months of unemployment were deep and lasting.

God spoke to her heart that she was not to pray for the JOB but rather for God's PROMISE. Day after day she <u>learned not to lean on her own understanding or opinion but to trust in God with all her heart</u>. *Proverbs 3:5-6* became her daily counsel*: "Trust in the Lord with all your heart and lean not on your own understanding. In all your ways acknowledge Him and He will direct your path."* She came to know peace daily as she began to learn how God Himself was to be her Provider and how deep was His love for her and His faithfulness to her.

Since I too was interceding for her during this time, I had to learn these old but tremendous lessons: **LET GO AND LET GOD. TRUST AND OBEY, FOR THERE'S NO OTHER WAY.**

And, of course, God brought her into the job (the field) He had been preparing her for right before her savings were exhausted. Once again, it proved true that God rarely is early in answering our prayers, but He never is late.

One verse that I've held tightly to over many years of intercession is **Hebrews 7:25.**

"Therefore <u>He is able also to save to the uttermost</u> (completely, perfectly, finally, and for all time and eternity) those who come to God through Him, since <u>He is always living to make petition to God and intercede with Him and intervene for them</u>."

So whatever you are interceding for, know this: Our Lord hears you and He's got this! We may not see the results we are expecting in the way or timing we want, but we can be assured that our prayers will be answered for all eternity. Almighty God can always be trusted.

11. Now take a moment to reflect on what you mentioned you were interceding for in question 8. Do you have expectations that you feel you need to surrender? <u>Can you trust God that He will answer your prayers according to His will</u>? Make a declaration here.

_____

_____

_____

_____

_____

_____

Chapter 2:
The Role of the Holy Spirit

"Leaning on Our Ever-present Helper"

The Holy Spirit comes to us...

It's such good news that Jesus, the Great High Priest, is seated at the right hand of Almighty God interceding on our behalf according to **Hebrews 7:25**. But how do we (on Earth) get our hearts connected to our Great High Priest when He's actually in heaven?

Before Jesus left this world, He told His disciples, *"You heard Me tell you I am going away and I am coming (back to you)." John 14:28* What a wonderful day that will be when Jesus returns for us, His beloved bride, Maranatha! But what does He expect us to do until then with all the cares of this world? John the Baptist revealed this about Jesus: *"But He Who is coming after me is mightier than I, Whose sandals I am not worthy or fit to take off or carry; He will baptize you with the Holy Spirit and with fire." Matthew 3:11b* After His work on Earth, Jesus left us His words and deeds to follow as an example, but He left us even more; God sent us the Holy Spirit Himself to dwell in us and to help us live victoriously until we see our Savior face to face.

In *Ephesians 1:13-14* Paul explains how we *"were stamped with the seal of the long-promised Holy Spirit. That Spirit is the guarantee of our inheritance (the firstfruits, the pledge and foretaste, the down payment on our heritage)..."* Then in *I Corinthians 6:19* we are asked, *"Do you not know that your body is the temple (the very sanctuary) of the Holy Spirit Who lives within you, Whom you have received (as a Gift) from God? You are not your own. You were bought with a price (purchased with a preciousness and paid for, made His own). So then, honor God and bring glory to Him in your body."*

Before Jesus left His disciples, He instructed them, *"But you shall receive power (ability, efficiency, and might) when the Holy Spirit has come upon you, and you shall be My witnesses in Jerusalem and all Judea and Samaria and to the ends (the very bounds) of the earth." Acts 1:8 "And after waiting for Pentecost, they experienced the outpouring of the Holy Spirit "And they were all filled (diffused throughout their souls) with the Holy Spirit and began to speak in other (different, foreign) languages (tongues), as the Spirit kept giving them clear and loud expression." Acts 2:4* That is how the first church was born, and that is still available to us today.

1. Do you have a daily relationship with the gentle Holy Spirit? If so, describe what He does for you. If not, why not ask to know His presence every day.

_____

_____

_____

_____

Who the Holy Spirit is...

The Holy Spirit is a Person, and He can be talked to like that. He is an essential part of the Trinity, the One that the Father gives to all who believe in His Son. He never seeks the glory for Himself because He is a true Gentleman. Jesus said in *John 14:24-25 "I have told you these things while I'm still with you. But the Comforter (Counselor, Helper, Intercessor, Advocate, Strengthener, Standy), the Holy Spirit, whom the Father will send in my name (in my place, to represent Me and act on My behalf), He will teach you all things. And He will cause you to recall (will remind you of, bring to your remembrance), everything I have told you."* He is also our Teacher, Guide, and Healer., and He is the One Who convicts us of sin and shows us a better way. *"And when He comes, He will convict and convince the world and bring demonstration to it about sin and about righteousness (uprightness of heart and right standing with God)..." John 16:8* He is all we need in life and He lives in us.

Have you ever thought what an amazing promise and provision this is for us and yet how He is rarely talked about even in Christian circles? Years ago there was an outpouring of the Holy Spirit with the Charismatic Movement, but in some cases this brought misunderstanding and division. However, the Holy Spirit comes to dwell in us at the moment we are saved, and we are to learn to recognize His presence and cling to Him for help in every way.

At times when we are perplexed or troubled and feeling desperate to talk with a friend, we don't really have to go far. There is a Person within us Who is always near to help: our personal Counselor and Standby. The Holy Spirit in us helps us to intercede for someone or something, especially if the burden is very intense and we are at a loss for how God could intervene or how we should even pray. *Romans 8:26-27 explains: "So too the Holy Spirit comes to our aid and bears us up in our weakness; for we do not know what prayer to offer nor how to offer it worthily as we ought, but the Spirit Himself goes to meet our supplication and pleads in our behalf with unspeakable yearnings and groaning too deep for utterance. And He Who searches the hearts of men knows what is in the mind of the Holy Spirit (what His intent is), because the Spirit intercedes and pleads (before God) in behalf of the saints according to and in harmony with God's will."* That's why there's such power in praying in the Spirit and why we should use our prayer language often. *Jude 1:20 "But you, beloved, build yourselves up (founded) on your most holy faith (make progress, rise like an edifice higher and higher), <u>praying in the Holy Spirit</u>."*

2. Describe a time when you did not know how to pray so you depended completely on the Holy Spirit and how it made you feel.

_____

_____

_____

_____

_____

_____

> **My hope in this chapter is that you might come to know and appreciate the different aspects of the Holy Spirit more fully and to recognize when you are walking in the Spirit.**

Living in the flesh or in the Spirit...

When we were first saved and the Holy Spirit joined with our spirits, <u>we received the fullness of all He is</u>. Although the nine fruit of the Spirit was deposited in us, it matures as we do and takes time to be fully manifested in our lives. *Galatians 5:22-23: "But the fruit of the (Holy) Spirit (the work which His presence within accomplishes) is <u>love, joy</u> (gladness), <u>peace, patience</u> (an even temper, forbearance), <u>kindness, goodness</u> (benevolence), <u>faithfulness, gentleness</u> (meekness, humility), <u>self-control</u> (self-restraint, continence)."* How wonderful it would be if we all enjoyed life with this fruit every day, but we have to learn how to think and live this way.

Each day, perhaps many times each day, we choose to walk in the flesh or in the Spirit. *Romans 8:5-6* explains how we live. *"For those who are <u>according to the flesh</u> and are controlled by its unholy desires set their minds on and pursue those things which gratify the flesh, but those who are according to the Spirit and are controlled by the <u>desires of the Spirit</u> <u>set their minds on and seek those things which gratify the (Holy) Spirit</u>. Now the mind of the flesh (which is sense and reason without the Holy Spirit) is death (death that comprises all the miseries arising from sin, both here and hereafter). But the mind of the (Holy) Spirit is life and (soul) peace (both now and forever)."*

There are three sources that try to hinder our walking in the Spirit: our flesh (or natural thinking and carnal desires), the world's ways, and Satan's deceptive strategies. As we grow in Christ, we should begin to recognize which of these sources is influencing us. As our understanding increases, we learn to turn from these influences and to walk and pray according to the Holy Spirit's leading.

Years ago I began to know the Holy Spirit as my Counselor. It was a difficult and intensely emotional time in my life, and He began to teach me how to deal with anger and other upsetting emotions. I began to assess what I was feeling, to give it a label or description beyond just anger. For example, I began to learn that underneath anger were the more painful feelings of fear or extreme sorrow, which I was feeling but trying to avoid. Then I saw that I had these feelings because of what I was thinking. God wanted to show me how to live in the Spirit rather than being controlled by the natural thinking of my flesh. I began to learn I didn't have to live according to my feelings; God wanted me instead to learn how to live according to His truth.

For example, I was angry at my husband because he was making negative choices that were hugely affecting our family. However, it wasn't his choices really that made me angry. It was rather my perspective, my own thinking that upset me. Beneath my anger, I was *afraid* of his rejection or abandonment and *sorrowful* because of the great loss his withdrawal was causing. Those may have been logical feelings considering his actions, but God was asking me to surrender my thinking to Him. In order not to be controlled by my flesh, I had to repent of my self-focused conclusions, my own grief, insecurities and fears, and ask God to speak His truth into my heart in order to transform my mind.

God began to show me His perspective and powerful promises from His Word that would encourage me. I gained peace of mind and security as I contemplated verses like ***Hebrews 13:6 "...for He (God) Himself has said, I will not in any way fail you nor give you up nor leave you without support. (I will) not, (I will) not, (I will) not in any degree leave you helpless nor forsake nor let (you) down (relax My hold on you!) (Assuredly not!)*** Once I received God truth into my heart, I found peace and was able to endure my husband's actions with more patience although my circumstances did not change immediately. I'd like to add here that now I *know* it is possible and even God's will that we live with hope, peace, and joy every day despite our very uncomfortable circumstances. However, we have to ask, believe, and receive this truth.

Later I learned that this process was being used by therapists and was known by some as *Misbelief Therapy*. It was talked about in William Backus' book called *Telling Yourself the Truth* and others. Currently there is much Christian and scientific teaching on the role of how dangerous toxic thinking is to our health and our lives. Now we know it is possible for us to get free of feelings like anxiety and fear even when they've been wired into our brains for years. There is great hope because science is proving our brains can be re-wired to bring us into peace. Two books I recommend are *Switch on Your Brain* by Dr. Carolyn Leaf and *The Rewired Brain* by Dr. Ski Chilton. If you find yourself struggling with destructive thinking, there is great hope. But remember it's a process; changing a negative thought into a positive one takes at least 21 days of repeating the truth and even more if it is deeply wired into your brain. Never give up letting God renew your mind; with Him all things are possible.

3. How have you experienced the Holy Spirit as your Counselor, Comforter or Helper? And which of the fruits of the Spirit do you want to experience most today?

_____

_____

_____

_____

_____

Transforming our mind and soul...

Our walk in the Spirit can be hindered by our flesh or natural thinking, by the ways of the world and our circumstances, or by Satan and his demonic strategies. ***John 13:2*** explains how Judas was led to betray Jesus, the One He served. ***"So it was during supper, Satan having already put the thought of betraying Jesus in the heart of Judas Iscariot, Simon's son."*** We might need to ask God for greater discernment if we are unsure what is tempting us or causing us to go astray. Each of these sources calls for a different response from us; for example, we might need to repent (change our thinking), once again consecrate ourselves to God, or resist the enemy (by rejecting his lies). We have Someone Who can help us know how to pray and walk in a way that pleases God. ***I Corinthians 2:13*** advises us ***"And we are setting these truths forth in words not taught by human wisdom but taught by the Holy Spirit, combining and interpreting spiritual truths with spiritual language (to those who possess the Holy Spirit)."*** The clearest advice is ***James 4:7-8*** ***"So be subject to God. Resist the devil (stand firm against him), and he will flee from you. Come close to God and He will come close to you."***

We need to pay attention to how our heart, our spirit, is doing daily. Taking a "fruit of the Spirit inventory" is a great practice. If we're honest with ourselves, we usually know right away when we are not full of love or peace or not acting kindly or with self-control. Moreover, it is good to begin to recognize the triggers or buttons that get pushed in our lives that cause us to lose our peace or our joy. We may from time to time experience any distressing emotion (like anger, fear or worry), but usually we tend to deal with one more than others. It is helpful for each of us to regularly evaluate our thoughts and feelings and to seek God's truth that will help us resist the enemy's strategies.

Romans 12:1-2 offers us good advice for dealing with troubling thoughts or emotions as well as for knowing the will of God in any situation. ***"I appeal to you (therefore, brethren, and beg of you in view of (all) the mercies of God, to make a decisive dedication of your bodies (*presenting al your members and faculties*) as a living sacrifice, holy (devoted, consecrated) and well pleasing to God, which is your reasonable (rational intelligent) *service and spiritual worship. Do not be conformed to this world* (this age), (fashioned after and adapted to its external, superficial customs), but *be transformed* (changed) by the (entire) renewal of your mind (by its new ideals and its new attitude), so that you may prove (for yourselves) what is the good and acceptable and perfect will of God, even the thing which is good and acceptable and perfect (in His sight for you)."***

Notice here that we have a choice of being conformed or transformed. We either join with the world (conform) or allow ourselves to connect with the mind of Christ (transform). We make this choice repeatedly each day. Our Christian journey should lead us to the place of becoming content, as the Apostle Paul was when he said, ***"for *I have learned how to be content* (satisfied to the point where I am not disturbed or disquieted) in whatever state I am." Philippians 4:11***

5. Since our brain is part of our body, it seems imperative that we make a decisive <u>dedication of that as a living sacrifice to God</u>. What thought or feeling do you need to present to God so that you might more clearly know His will in the matter?

_____

_____

_____

_____

_____

Typical enemies of our souls...

In ***Ephesians 4:30*** are advised, ***"And *do not grieve the Holy Spirit of God* (do not offend or vex or sadden Him), by whom you were sealed (marked, branded as God's own, secured) for the day of redemption (of final deliverance through Christ from evil and the consequences of sin)."*** Then again in ***I Thessalonians 5:19 we read, "*Do not quench (suppress or subdue) the Holy Spirit.*"*** We would do well to question how we might do that.

There could be many ways we grieve or quench the Holy Spirit, but perhaps it is our own thoughts that do this most often. When we hold onto our "fleshly" or "stinking" thinking, we may be blocking the Holy Spirit. <u>When we submit our thinking and depend on God, the Holy Spirit is released to transform</u> our minds, to change our focus and to re-wire our brain, causing our intercessory prayer to become more effective. Therefore, let us always strive to recognize and overcome undesirable feelings, such as the troublesome ones below, by changing our self-talk.

FEAR: This may be the most common and extensive negative emotion (just think of all the phobias people have). To begin to challenge fear, the most frequent and easily changeable thought is to <u>take "what if's" out of your vocabulary</u>. Whenever we think or say that, our thoughts inevitably spiral toward fear or dread.

TRUTH: Instead, talk truth and hope to yourself, convincing your soul that God loves you unconditionally and that His perfect love casts out fear. ***I John 4: 18-19: "There is <u>no fear in love</u> (dread does not exist), but full-grown (complete, perfect) <u>love turns fear out of doors</u> and expels every trace of terror! For fear brings with it the thought of punishment, and (so) <u>he who is afraid has not reached the full maturity of love</u> (is not yet grown into love's complete perfection). We love Him because He first loved us."***

5.   We might avoid years of therapy if (instead of <u>trying to be less fearful</u>) we decided to draw closer to God, the One who loves us so unconditionally, and to discover how much He really does love us. Think of a fear you have or a "what if" that often comes to your mind and record it here. Then ask God to begin to transform your mind so that you are able to know His love more deeply in this area.

_____

_____

_____

_____

_____

_____

WORRY/ANXIETY: Years ago I heard Bill Gothard give a great definition of worry: *"Worry is assuming a responsibility God never intended you to have."* I think God would like us to know those <u>things that we worry about are His responsibility,</u> under His control. Remember the wonderful verses in **Matthew chapter 6** where Jesus explains this. It begins right after He says we cannot serve two masters *(verse 24)* and ends by urging us not to think like the world does. But rather let us seek first of all His kingdom and His righteousness and then all the other things will be added to our lives (my paraphrase).

TRUTH: I believe God would quiet our anxious thoughts by simply saying, *"I've got this. Trust Me."* Before Jesus left this earth, he gave His disciples this encouragement that is actually a commandment: ***"Peace I leave with you; My (own) peace** I now give and bequeath to you. Not as the world gives do I give to you. **Do not let** your hearts be troubled, neither let them be afraid. **(Stop allowing yourselves to be agitated and disturbed;** and **do not permit yourselves to be fearful** and intimidated and cowardly and unsettled.) John 14:17.*

6. What thought often causes you to lose your peace, to worry or have anxiety? What is the worse that could possibly happen? Can you surrender that thought to God and ask Him to help you believe and trust Him more? Record your thought or thoughts here and hear what He would say in response.

_____

_____

_____

_____

_____

_____

There are many other enemies of our soul who try to harass us by invading our thoughts. See which of these causes you the most difficulty and follow the process mentioned above of surrendering your thoughts to be transformed by God's Word. Some of the most troubling are: **self-pity, confusion, doubt, despair, guilt, unforgiveness, shame, discouragement, and weariness.** If any of these often torment you, let me just say that you can put an end to their harassment. If God is in you, on your side, <u>you have the power to get free of these enemies</u>.

We have only to hold fast to the truth of ***Romans 8:31 "What then shall we say to all this? If God is for us, who can be against us? (Who can be our foe, if God is on our side?)"*** Another helpful reminder that bears audible personalized confession is ***"Who is there to condemn us? Will Christ Jesus (the Messiah), Who died, or rather Who was raised from the dead, who is at <u>the right hand of God actually pleading as He intercedes for us</u>?" (Romans 8:34)*** If He's on our side, nothing else really matters. We need our thinking to agree with His truth. Depend wholeheartedly on the Holy

Spirit in you to set you free and lead you into His way of peace and wholeness. And *never give up!* <u>God wants us to defeat the enemies that torment our soul, and He equips us to do just that through the power of His Holy Spirit</u>.

7. Explain here *why and how* you can defeat the enemies of your soul and live victoriously in Christ.

_____

_____

_____

_____

Peace, the umpire of our souls...

I like how Paul greeted people by writing, ***"<u>May grace (God's unmerited favor) and spiritual peace</u> (which means <u>peace with God and harmony, unity, and undisturbedness</u>) be yours from God our Father and from the Lord Jesus Christ." (Ephesians 1:2)*** Lately God has been alerting me to any moments when I do not feel at peace and leading me to deal with it. When we lack peace, we may not be walking in the Spirit since that is a key fruit of the Spirit.

I love the verse in ***Colossians 3:15*** in the Amplified Bible that sounds like it's an act of our will. ***"And <u>let the peace</u> (soul harmony which comes) from Christ rule (<u>act as umpire continually</u>) in your hearts (deciding and settling with finality all questions that arise in your minds, in that peaceful state) to which as (members of Christ's) one body you were also called (to live). And <u>be thankful (appreciative), giving praise to God always</u>.*** Since peace is to be an umpire of our soul, we are to be aware of any "foul balls" that are entering our minds. We don't have to accept every thought that comes our way from circumstances or even from our enemy. <u>We can refuse such thoughts and surrender them to Christ, which then causes us to be thankful</u>.

Through the power of the Holy Spirit in us, we can overcome negative thinking. Paul reminds us in ***II Corinthians 10:4-5 "For the <u>weapons of our warfare are not physical</u> (weapons of flesh and blood), but they are mighty before God for the overthrow and destruction of strongholds, (inasmuch as <u>we) refute arguments and theories and reasonings</u> and every proud and lofty thing that sets itself up against the (true) knowledge of God; and we lead every thought and purpose away captive into obedience of Christ (the Messiah, the Anointed One)."*** Let us never forget that Satan is a master deceiver, and we need to detect his lies and bring our thoughts into obedience with what is in Christ's mind.

8. Does something <u>come to your mind that causes you anxiety or fear</u>? If so, discuss it with God right here by identifying it and presenting it to God as a sacrifice. As you relinquish it, ask God to give you a new thought or Scripture to replace the other. This may be a long Holy-Spirit therapy session, but let the Spirit in you act as an umpire to remind you that your old negative thoughts are no longer accepted in your soul.

_____

_____

_____

_____

_____

_____

The weapon of rest...

Perhaps you know a lot already about spiritual warfare and know that the battlefield is usually in our minds. Here I want to emphasize that the Holy Spirit is with us to help us with any and all enemy attacks. So as we intercede for others, <u>it's essential that we never forget Christ's sacrifice and the power of the Holy Spirit in us</u>. God would have our faith be strong and unwavering so that we can hold fast to this promise in *Ephesians 3:20-21. Now to Him Who, by (in consequence of) the (action of <u>His) power that is at work within us,</u> is able to (carry our His purpose and) <u>do super-abundantly, far over and above all</u> that we (dare) ask or think (infinitely beyond our highest prayers, desires, thoughts, hopes, or dreams—To Him be glory in the church and in Christ Jesus throughout all generations forever and ever. Amen (so be it)."* Notice that this awesome promise is <u>in consequence of the action of His power at work</u> in us, in other words, the power of the Holy Spirit. So as we release the Holy Spirit in us, God is free to complete His marvelous work; and the result is our soul is at rest.

Hebrews 4:11 gives us the key to being at rest by reminding us that <u>our efforts should be in *believing* and *obeying*</u> rather than in our own works. *"Let us therefore be zealous and exert ourselves and <u>strive diligently to enter the rest</u> (of God, to know and experience it for ourselves), that no one may fall or perish by the same kind of unbelief and disobedience (into which those in the wilderness fell)."*

It is because of God's grace through our faith that we were saved to enjoy relationship with Him *(Ephesians 2:8-9),* and in much the same way, <u>that is how we enter His rest.</u> We expect (or <u>have faith</u>) that His grace will lead us into rest. God desires that we be <u>a channel for His love and grace</u>

to pass through, and that flow is blocked when we are not at rest. We cannot save a lost and dying world no matter how hard we pray; we cannot make a way where there is no way; and we cannot work together all the threads of our lives into good like He can. What we can do is partner with Him by faith. It is good to remember that answers to prayer are not our responsibility; they are God's. When we see that our prayers are simply connecting with the Father's heart, we come into rest and our intercession becomes easier and more effective.

While we are on this Earth we will face difficult circumstances and spiritual warfare, which always try to derail our daily peace, rob us of joy, and diminish the effectiveness of our intercession. For this reason, I highly recommend Graham Cooke's series of books that begins with *Qualities of a Spiritual Warrior*. On page 35 of that book Cooke writes: *"Rest is a weapon. As Christians, we should be incredibly peaceful, tranquil, and calm. The enemy cannot penetrate the armor of a person at rest in God. Spiritual warriors know that part of their inheritance is complete confidence in Him. This confidence in His nature puts their spirit at rest. All of God's promises are designed to inspire us in our dependence on Him. We are completely reliant on His grace and mercy. All we can do is joyfully and humbly live in that revelation no matter what comes against us."*

And again on page 38 he writes:

> *"To rest in God's power when your own weaknesses seem to be screaming at you—that's grace!*
>
> *To be confident in who God is for you when you feel overwhelmed by odds against you—that's peace!*
>
> *To stand alone against massive intimidation—that's trust!"*

On page 48 he sums up our role simply with **Psalm 46:10 "Be still and know that I am God."** Let us receive that word deeply in our souls.

Worshiping in intercession...

Intercession is birthed from true worship, but what does worship mean? Remember the phrase in **Romans 12:2** that says to present ourselves as a reasonable service and spiritual worship? Worship is not just singing but rather an attitude of heart-surrender to God. Notice the passage in **John 4** where a woman gives Jesus water to drink. After a time of dialogue, Jesus begins to explain to the woman what worship actually is. It is not dependent on being in a certain place **(verse 20-21)** but rather on understanding the role of spirit and truth. **"A time will come, however, indeed it is already here, when the true (genuine) worshipers will worship the Father in spirit and in truth (reality); for the Father is seeking just such people as these as His worshipers. God is a Spirit (a spiritual Being) and those who worship Him must worship Him in spirit and in truth (reality)." John 4:23-24**

As we have seen in this chapter, our intercession is to be <u>led by the Spirit and full of God's truth</u>. That's why I say that true worship is a key part of intercession. When we have a heart of worship, we are connecting with the Almighty God Himself. As we let go of ourselves, our thoughts and our reservations, we agree with the power of the Holy Spirit of Truth.

9.   With the *John 4* passage in mind, explain what you feel like during a time of true worship; then explain how this would help you intercede for what is on the Father's heart.

_____

_____

I think it's interesting that the <u>first mention of worship was in Genesis</u> when Abraham took God's promised son Isaac to be sacrificed. He told his servants: ***"Settle down and stay here with the donkey, and I and the young man will go yonder and <u>worship</u> and come again to you." See Genesis 22:5.*** Abraham was being <u>asked to sacrifice God's promised son, and yet he still considered this a time of worship</u>. Interesting… Worship doesn't always involve music; it's more an attitude of willingness, a heart issue. Abraham had every <u>intention of obeying</u> God, but He also showed <u>great faith</u> when he said they would "come again to see you." God was looking at Abraham's heart and intent, and his obedience pleased God. He then intervened and provided a ram to become the sacrifice.

<u>Worship is a heart attitude of sacrifice and faith</u>. It is a great privilege and a powerful tool for intercession <u>because it brings our hearts into a position of surrender or yielding to the will of God</u>. It also affords us the opportunity to make bold declarations of faith, and the power of music makes that even more emphatic.

I can recall many times when I was troubled while <u>facing difficult situations that "out of the blue" a song or hymn came to my mind</u>, perhaps one I had not heard for many years. For example, I had been my mother's caretaker for twelve years and loved her dearly, but it was becoming clear that her Alzheimer's disease was getting too severe and that I would need to move her away from me, to place which could better meet her needs. I was troubled about what to do until one day after school, when I wasn't even praying, my soul heard clearly this old hymn "Be Still My Soul," and the words set my hurting heart free. I'm going to transcribe all three verses here (as they are sung to the old "Finlandia") because they may be equally powerful to you.

> **"Be still, my soul; the Lord is on your side. Bear patiently the cross of grief or pain; leave to your God to order and provide; in every change God faithful will remain. Be still, my soul, your best, your heavenly friend through thorny ways leads to a joyful end.**

Be still, my soul; your God will undertake to guide the future as in ages past. Your hope, your confidence let nothing shake; all now mysterious shall be bright at last. Be still my soul, the waves and winds still know the Christ who ruled them while he dwelt below.

Be still, my soul; the hour is hastening on when we shall be forever with the Lord, when disappointment, grief, and fear are gone, sorrow forgot, love's purest joys restored. Be still, my soul; when change and tears are past, all safe and blessed we shall meet at last."

10. Was there a part of this hymn that really spoke to you? Or has the Holy Spirit ever put a song in your heart? If so explain that here or talk about a favorite song that's a powerful declaration for you.

_____

_____

_____

_____

The Holy Spirit's anointing and power...

In the Old Testament, we read of the prophets anointing the one who was to be king. The use of this oil set apart those who were chosen for God's holy purposes. *Psalm 105:15* shows how God protects those He anoints *"Saying, <u>Touch not My anointed</u>, and do My prophets no harm."* Then again in *Psalm 20:6 "Now I know that the <u>Lord saves His anointed</u>; He will answer him from His Holy heaven with the saving strength of His right hand."*

I believe <u>when we are walking in the Holy Spirit, following His lead in whatever He calls us to do, we are moving in God's anointing</u>. When our soul is still or at rest in Christ, we can be assured that God's anointing in on us. Then we are able to hear more clearly what God has to say, and we are more aware of His power and His grace. Our faith increases, and it's easier to obey and intercede as the Spirit leads us. *"But <u>you have been anointed</u> by (you hold a sacred appointment from, you have been given an unction from) the Holy One, and you all know the Truth or you know all things." I John 2:20* Then again in *verse 27*, John writes *"But as for you, <u>the anointing</u> (the sacred appointment, the unction) which you received from Him <u>abides permanently in you</u>; so then you have no need that anyone should instruct you. But just as <u>His anointing teaches you concerning everything and is true and is no falsehood</u>, so you must abide in (live in, never depart from) Him (being rooted in Him, knit to Him) just as His anointing has taught you to do."*

A good verse to remember when facing difficulties in any situation is **Revelation 12:11 *"And they have overcome (conquered) him by means of the blood of the Lamb, and by the utterance of their testimony, for they did not love and cling to life…"*** At times of enemy attack, we are to remember that the power of Christ's blood really is enough. It is our responsibility *to believe and declare this and stay close to the only One* who paid the full price, surrendering our own thoughts and opinions. Our <u>confession of faith in Him stops the enemy in his tracks and makes our intercession more effective</u>.

As we discussed earlier, it's crucial not to linger in a state of weariness or with feelings of condemnation, doubt or unforgiveness as they can hinder the work of the Holy Spirit. When we feel overwhelmed, we may need to go to trusted prayer partners in the body of Christ. Satan will try to isolate us, and that often deepens the problem. Even though our Counselor is always with us, ministering to our inner needs, sometimes He chooses to work through others. When it's too hard, reach out to others who can come alongside you, encourage you, and help you as well. Jesus advises this: ***"Again I tell you, <u>if two of you on earth agree</u> (harmonize together, make a symphony together) about whatever (anything and everything) they may ask, it will come to pass and be done for them by My Father in heaven." Matthew 19:19*** But may I add, that with the Holy Spirit in you, you are never alone.

<u>The Holy Spirit is always ready to comfort us and to anoint us with the oil of joy</u> that is able to transform every person. ***Isaiah 61:3 "To grant (consolation and joy) to those who mourn in Zion— to give them an ornament (a garland or diadem) of beauty instead of ashes, <u>the oil of joy instead of mourning, the garment of praise instead of a heavy, burdened, and failing spirit</u>—that they may be called oaks of righteousness (lofty, strong, and magnificent, distinguished for uprightness, justice, and right standing with God), the planting of the Lord, <u>that He may be glorified</u>."***

The Holy Spirit is with us always, standing by to help whenever we call out to Him. He is the One who draws us nearer to the heart of God. He is our Counselor and Teacher and leads us into all Truth. He is an essential part of all our intercession as He is the One who understands what's on our heart (even more than we do) and who brings it to Jesus, our Advocate.

He brings comfort to our soul in every time of distress, and He is our constant Helper, bringing us grace and mercy in our times of need. All that we need to do is come boldly before His throne of grace, ***"the throne of God's unmerited favor to us sinners that we may receive mercy (for our failures) and <u>find grace to help</u> in good time for every need (appropriate help and well-timed help, coming just when we need it)." (Hebrews 4:20)***

11. What do you think it means to be anointed to do something? Explain how God anoints us to serve Him and to intercede.

_____

_____

_____

_____

_____

_____

Chapter 3:
Called to Your Field

"Learning to Bloom Where You Are Planted"

Recognize where your fields have been...

As we grow in intercession, we will begin to recognize that God puts us in situations or certain fields in order to touch that part of the world with His presence. <u>Your field is another way to refer to your sphere of influence, the people and situations closest to you</u>. The longer we serve the Lord, the more we see how God doesn't waste anything. He uses all that happens to us in life: the good, the bad, and even the ugly. If you have begun to see yourself as an intercessor, you might be wondering *who* or *what* God would have be the focus of your intercession right now.

Does God really care about where we live, where we work, or where we go to church? Most people would say, "Of course He cares." But not all of us have looked back on our lives, reflecting on places or situations we've been in, and seen how God <u>sovereignly planted</u> us in cities, in neighborhoods, at work places, and with certain groups of people. He desires to use us as intercessors wherever we are in order to connect others to the Father's heart of love. ***John 15:16 "You have not chosen Me, but I have chosen you, and <u>I have appointed you (I have planted you)</u>, that <u>you might go and bear fruit</u> and keep on bearing, and that your fruit may be lasting (that it may remain, abide), so that whatever you ask the Father is My Name (as presenting all that I AM), He may give it to you."***

Some may refer to this "sovereign planting" as fate, and they argue that mankind has been given free will. Although that is true, <u>God has a way of putting desires in our hearts as well as opening and closing doors in order to fulfill His plans or purposes</u>. If we are seeking His will, He tends to bring us, His people, to the places where He would plant us for each season of our lives. Where God takes us may be our heart's desire or it may be a disappointment or uncomfortable. But, as we will see, God will always use it and be with us while we are there. Could it be that the all-wise and almighty God has allowed things to happen in our lives for His purposes, which may or may not be revealed to us this side of heaven?

1. Think of a place where you were for a season that seemed to be a big mistake. Has God shown you how He plans to use this time in your life? If so, please explain.

    _____

    _____

    _____

    _____

Why do you think God allows us to get into difficult situations? Could it be that He knows best how to conform us to His image? A great passage to study that brings light on this subject and reminds us of the bigger picture of life is ***Romans, chapter 8.*** Why not take a few minutes and meditate on that whole chapter? Notice ***verse 28: "We are assured and know that (God being a partner in their labor) <u>all things work together and are (fitting into a plan) for good</u> to and for those who love God and are called according to (His) design and purpose." Romans 8:28*** has been my "life verse" because, although my life has not gone at all like I had hoped or expected, God has always been with me, working in me and working out His will for me. I've seen many of my life's pieces fit together, and now I'm convinced there will be a lovely picture when the tapestry of my life is revealed. I just need <u>more of an eternal perspective to keep from getting bogged down with all the loose (and sometimes ugly) threads of my life</u>.

The first step to understanding your "field" is to recognize what or where it is. My hope is that by looking back and reflecting on past experiences, you will gain a profound appreciation for the field you find yourself in currently.

---

2. Think back over the major events of your life and list 3-5 fields (or key places/situations) that you have experienced. Then after each try to explain how God might possibly have used the time you spent in each, that is, explain possible eternal meaning or significance each may have for you or for those around you.

    Field #1 _____ Significance:

    _____

    _____

    Field #2 _____ Significance:

    _____

    _____

Field #3 _____ Significance:

_____

_____

Field #4 _____ Significance:

_____

_____

Field #5 _____ Significance:

_____

_____

Perhaps you are like me and would like to delete a few places (or situations) from your memory. Remember sometimes it's the black threads that make the tapestry radiate life and depth. Perhaps you know you went out of God's will for a season; that is when you can thank God for your Redeemer who truly can work all things together for your good.

We need always to remember that even if we may take detours from God's will and find ourselves in some pretty difficult situations, <u>God never leaves us. His cord of love stays attached to us</u>, to someday draw us back to His will. Immanuel means God with us, and He takes care of those He loves and uses everything we go through to transform us in to His image, for His ultimate glory.

Being content in each of your fields...

Perhaps you're looking back over your life, as I was, with great wonder and awe, catching glimpses of why God chose to plant you where He did. Perhaps you can see the growth in you as a person, or as an intercessor, that was brought about largely by situations (jobs, marriages, neighborhoods, etc.) that may have been God-selected for you.

One lesson I've learned in a few situations is that <u>we may not be released from a difficult situation until we learn to be content in it</u>. For example, as a teacher I was in a public school where everyone seemed to be uncomfortably different from me. How I longed for the days where I was able to find even one person that I felt held similar values as mine. I prayed that God would open up another school for me, and so I applied to schools where I thought it would be better. After a good time of prayer one day, I came away spontaneously singing *"**You shall go out with joy and be led forth with peace**," (Isaiah 55:12)* I knew that was a Spirit song, <u>so I immediately assumed God was taking me</u>

from that field, to my great joy. However, months dragged on, until one day the Lord quickened this understanding to me. I felt Him say, "I never meant I was leading you forth at that time, just that WHEN I do, it will be with joy and peace."

God never seems to release us from situations until we learn whatever lesson He has for us. God will never lead us where His grace cannot keep us, but we do need to expect that grace and even call out for it in faith. Moreover, God's grace gives us favor with others in sometimes very difficult situations. Favor means approval, support or liking, and God's grace can bring us the favor we need. It's always good to ask God *into* our circumstances rather than asking to get *out* of them. Often we must learn to love the people who are there, especially when they are different from us. His heart is for *all people* not just for *our comfort*. **Romans 5:8** explains God's love for even the unlovable people around us. **"But God shows and _clearly proves His (own) love for us_ by the fact that _while we were still sinners_, Christ (the Messiah, the Anointed One) died for us."**

So I learned to appreciate where I was planted, to be careful not to judge, to grow in understanding the people around me, and to see more of why God may have wanted me there, Before too long another door opened and I was released to go to another school. Then I was led forth with peace and with great joy in knowing I had completed God's assignment in that last place. And, interestingly, I knew I was actually going to miss those people. I had learned to appreciate and even love them.

An intercessor's role is to connect the natural to the supernatural, to bring our situations to God, and to trust Him to be with us at all times. In fact, even when facing and overcoming difficult situations (abuse, divorce, death etc.), many can testify that they have gained a great deal from their time of suffering. I like Joyce Meyer's statement that there can be no *test*imony without a *test*. When we surrender to God, He can change our hearts and do wonderful things during times of trial. Where we allow our hearts to be most deeply touched, a connection is made to the heart of God. Every pain we endure becomes a touch-point to our Father's heart of love and compassion. So when our trials make us better instead of bitter, we gain Kingdom authority that helps us intercede for others in that same area with great power and purpose. I believe God would use us wherever He would plant us, and that He may ask us some day if we learned more about how to love while we were there.

3. Let's think now about a certain situation where you know you weren't always comfortable, but where you interceded for someone or something.

   Where were you planted? _____

   For whom or how were you interceding? _____

   Were you able to see any results to your prayers or is that for later?

   _____

   _____

The importance of limiting your field...

Before Jesus left this earth to return to His heavenly home, He interceded for His disciples. The entire chapter of ***John 17*** is a beautiful prayer by the obedient Son to His Father, Whose will He always sought to do. As we become more like Jesus, perhaps we will find ourselves speaking in a similar way at the end of our earthly journey.

First let's notice ***verse 6: "I have manifested Your Name (I have revealed Your very Self, Your real Self) to the <u>people whom You have given me</u> out of the world. They were Yours, and You gave them to Me, and they have obeyed and kept Your word."*** Then again in ***verse 9: "I am praying for them. I am not praying (requesting) for the world, but for <u>those You have given Me, for they belong to You</u>."*** Since God knows the future, He knows who belongs to Him. Our job is simply to help those who are in our field and to pray for them. Our enemy may try to side-track us with other "good" tasks and needs, but we must be careful to limit our fields to those God has put in our lives or on our hearts.

Notice also ***verse 20: "Neither for these alone do I pray (it is not for their sake only that I make this request), but also <u>for all those who will ever come to believe</u> in (trust in, cling to, rely on) Me through their word and teaching."*** Here we can see that the results of our prayers could go beyond certain persons to all those who are touched by *their* lives. Our job is to let the light of God's love warm the hearts of all around us; and one day in heaven, <u>we may be surprised how large our field actually was</u>.

The world's needs may seem overwhelming, but there may be one aspect or people group that stirs your heart the most. You can always ask God to make it clear who or what you are to bring before the throne of grace and ask for God's intervention. He loves to direct our intercession in every field where we are planted. The purpose of our intercession may always be to draw others into a deeper relationship with Father, that they might experience eternal life. ***John 17:3 "And this is eternal life: (it means) to know (to perceive, recognize, become acquainted with and understand) You, the only true and real God, and (likewise) to know Him, Jesus (as the) Christ (the Anointed one, the Messiah), whom You have sent."***

4.   Keeping in mind the verses in ***John 17***, list a few people or matters that you feel God would have you pray for. Is there a promise He's giving you for each one?

1) _____

_____

2) _____

_____

3) _____

_____

As I emphasized before, our intercession should never be a heavy burden that weighs us down or discourages us. (It might even energize us!) We must remember we are simply joining our prayers to those of the great High Priest and the Holy Spirit Who are both constantly <u>interceding for us and with us that the Father's will be done.</u>

Interceding as salt and light...

Perhaps you don't feel very connected to the people around you in the field where you are currently planted. As a teacher in a public school, I often felt frustrated that I was not allowed to speak of my faith or bring parents and students to see the best Answer to their problems. Have you ever wondered, "Why am I here, Lord, and what am I able to do or say?"

I think God would answer our heart questions like this by simply saying, "It's not so much what you do or say. <u>It's just that you are there</u>. Trust Me. I use all that concerns you." It's sometimes hard for us to remember we are human *beings*, not *doings*. One time I sensed the Lord telling me, "*Stop doing and **be**, vitally connected to Me.*"

In **Matthew 5** Jesus was telling his disciples and others how they could be blessed and happy because of certain conditions: the poor in spirit, those who mourn, the meek, those who hunger and thirst for righteousness, the merciful, the pure in heart, the peacemakers, and the persecuted. Then He went on to explain WHO they were, not so much what they were to say and do. ***Matthew 5:13-16** says "<u>You are the salt</u> of the earth, but if salt has lost its taste (its strength its quality), how can its saltiness be restored? It is not good for anything any longer but to be thrown out and trod underfoot by men. <u>You are the light</u> of the world. A city set on a hill cannot be hidden...Let your light so shine before men that they may see your moral excellence and your praiseworthy, noble and good deeds and recognize and honor and praise and glorify your Father Who is in heaven."*

<u>So maybe it's our life itself</u>, the values we hold and the excellence of all we do, <u>that impacts our field most and serves as our intercession</u>. What do salt and light actually do? They don't produce actions but their presence makes a great difference. It's our presence as well as our prayers that can make a huge difference. We can make situations more flavorful (as salt does to food) and bring light into dark places perhaps simply by our optimism, lack of criticism, or laughter. A person filled with the Holy Spirit will impact a place just as salt and light transform without even trying. When our hearts are tightly connected to the Father's heart, we are bringing hope to the hopeless, love to the lovable and unlovable alike, just by our daily responses and attitudes.

5.   How might you have been "salt" in a situation or relationship?

_____

_____

_____

Where was a dark place or time where you might have brought light?

_____

_____

_____

6.   Describe your current field .That is, where are you or what is on your heart most often? Describe how your presence alone might have an impact on others.

_____

_____

_____

_____

_____

The intercessor's challenge...

Hebrews 12:1-3 is a powerful picture of the Christian journey, but it is especially pertinent for us as intercessors. Sometimes our intercession requires great endurance; it's often a marathon rather than a sprint.

"Therefore then, since we are surrounded by so great a cloud of witnesses (who have borne testimony to the Truth), <u>let us strip off and throw aside every encumbrance</u> (unnecessary weight) and that sin which so readily (deftly and cleverly) clings to and entangles us, and <u>let us run with patient endurance and steady and active persistence</u> the appointed course of the race that is set before us, <u>looking away (from all that will distract) to Jesus,</u> Who is the Leader and the

Source of our faith (giving the first incentive for our belief) and is also its Finisher (bringing it to maturity and perfection). He, for the joy (of obtaining the prize) that was set before Him, endured the cross, despising and ignoring the shame, and is now seated at the right hand of the throne of God. Just think of Him Who endured from sinners such grievous opposition and bitter hostility against Himself (reckon up and consider it all in comparison with your trials), so that you may not grow weary or exhausted, losing heart and relaxing and fainting in your minds." (Hebrews 12:1-3)

7. After reading this passage in Hebrews, explain the following...

Who do you think is included in the cloud of witnesses?

_____

What are some weights that you may need to strip off?

_____

_____

_____

What is the course of the race set before you?

_____

_____

Where must you keep your focus?

_____

What tends to distract you?

_____

_____

_____

Why might you grow weary and what should you do then?

_____

_____

_____

Notice how this passage uses the phrase "fainting in your minds." Remember all that was discussed in Chapter 2 about how our thoughts and feelings affect us. Our physical actions and weariness are often the result of what's going on in our minds. Of course, we must always take care of ourselves physically by sleeping enough and eating well, but we are to be aware of our thoughts and feelings and keep our minds renewed daily.

Remember the encouragement in **Romans 12** to present ourselves daily to God and allow Him to renew our minds. It is the power of the Holy Spirit and the Word of God that helps us to re-wire our thinking and thereby gain the mind of Christ.

When the marathon of life begins to feel too long or too hard, the Holy Spirit is always there to encourage and strengthen us. A key to our successful "marathon" is explained in **II Corinthians 10:5.** This is actually a command that enables us to live more victoriously. We are able to keep our focus by daily thinking about what we are thinking about and *"Casting down vain imaginations and every high thing that exalts itself against the perfect will of God, and bringing our thoughts into captivity to the obedience of Christ." (my paraphrase)* That is, as Joyce Meyer's would say, "Get rid of our stinking thinking as soon as it happens." Some Christians don't realize we can reject any thought that disrupts our peace and confidence, and God expects us to do just that.

Preparing the field before planting seeds...

The field you are in right now may not immediately be ready for planting crops and bringing forth a harvest. Sometimes our role in a certain field is just to plow the ground, to loosen hardened soil, or to remove stones, boulders, and garbage that has been buried for years. Another person may be sent to that field to scatter seeds, remove weeds, or water plants. In fact, it's a special privilege when we see the fruit of our labors or a harvest being reaped.

Perhaps a person you are interceding for needs to go through a season of inner healing or counseling before they are ready to receive words of hope and truth. Perhaps during that time you are able to help them work through issues or maybe you are simply to bring them before the throne of grace, to find mercy and help in their time of need. See **Hebrews 4:16 *"Let us then fearlessly and confidently and boldly draw near to the throne of grace (the throne of God's unmerited favor to us*** *sinners), that we may <u>receive mercy (for our failures) and find grace to help in good time for every need</u> (appropriate help, and well-timed help, coming just when you need it).*

8. Mention a time when you knew you were plowing the ground for future work of the Holy Spirit or helping others to weed or deal with garbage in people's hearts. Explain how what was happening then may have been a work of intercession.

_____

_____

_____

_____

Sowing seeds of truth and life...

Matthew 13 describes how the Word is sowed onto four types of soil; only when the soil of a person's heart is ready, can the seed bloom and grow. The Father knows each person's heart better than they do and He knows when the heart is ready. Our role is not to force seed to grow, but to faithfully sow and water the seed. And to never give up!

We've all heard of the principle of sowing and reaping in terms of sin..."you reap what you sow." And we've also heard of it in terms of sowing financially into God's Kingdom. But have you ever measured your prayers in these terms? What have you sowed over the years in prayer? Have you allowed love to be planted in many hearts because of your prayers and acts of love? *Galatians 6:7-9 says, "...For <u>whatever a man sows that and that only is what he will reap</u>....he who sows to the Spirit will from the Spirit reap eternal life...And <u>let us not lose heart and grow weary and faint</u> in acting nobly and doing right, for in due time and at the <u>appointed season we shall reap</u>, if we do not loosen and relax our courage and faint."*

Let's think a minute further about what seeds we plant. When we receive a Word or Promise from God, it's important that <u>we intercede by declaring that Word out loud</u>, perhaps numerous times. Doing this is planting seeds of truth in the atmosphere. *Ephesians 3:10 says "(The purpose is) that through the church the complicated, many-sided wisdom of God in all its infinite variety and innumerable aspects <u>might now be made known to the angelic rulers and authorities (principalities and powers) in the heavenly sphere</u>."*

Furthermore, whenever we speak a negative word or refuse to see things from another person's point of view, we are planting <u>seeds of discord and division, and releasing that into the atmosphere.</u> That's what, at some point in time, we will harvest: more discord or division. This law of nature and planting affects all of our lives. *We will reap what we sow.* Plant words of love: forgiveness, hope or understanding, and these are the qualities you will harvest in that relationship. It may take time before a healthy harvest is produced. It may take many seeds and much care, but this law is absolute. Plant seeds of God's unconditional love, and you will reap that same love in God's perfect timing.

The Kingdom principle of "What you sow, you will reap," means to me that if we are full of God's peace through His Holy Spirit, whatever we plant in our prayers, must come to fruition. Just as in the natural when we plant corn, ears of *corn* (not carrots or radishes) must begin to grow. Likewise, when we plant seeds of love and the truth of God's Word in the spiritual ground of prayer and intercession, there must be a harvest of that love and truth waiting for us someday...It's inevitable! Consider the **Beatitudes of Matthew 5.** The verse saying **"Blessed are the merciful, for they shall obtain mercy (verse 7)** could be paraphrased: If you plant seeds of mercy in others' lives, you will reap mercy when you need it. This is an absolute principle in God's Kingdom, and this gives us great confidence in our intercession.

What are some seeds you may be sowing in your relationships or in your prayers: love, hope, respect, forgiveness, grace, beauty, kindness, gentleness, joy, peace, encouragement, courage?

9. Why not take a few minutes to reflect on what seeds you are currently sowing in your intercession?

_____

_____

What do you see as the inevitable fruit to be reaped some day because of your prayers?

_____

_____

Whatever the purpose of where we are right now (for plowing, planting, or harvesting) it's important that we are faithful to continue and not get discouraged or impatient to see results.

Pruning for fruitfulness...

In concluding this section about the fields God calls us to, I'd like to focus on the beautiful passage *of John 15:1-4 "I am the True Vine, and My Father is the Vinedresser. Any branch in Me that does not bear fruit (that stops bearing) He cuts away (trims off, takes away); and He cleanses and repeatedly prunes every branch that continues to bear fruit, to make it bear more and richer and more excellent fruit. You are cleansed and pruned already, because of the word which I* *have given you (the teachings I have discussed with you). Dwell in Me, and I will dwell in you. (Live in Me, and I will live in you) Just as no branch can bear fruit of itself without abiding in (being vitally united to) the vine, <u>neither can you bear fruit unless you abide in Me</u>.*" This is not talking about people being pruned out of God's kingdom, but rather it's about the <u>thoughts</u> we have or <u>actions</u> we do that may not be productive or result in bearing any of the fruit of the Spirit listed in *Galatians 522.*

In the passage from *John 15,* Jesus reminds us that He is the vine and we are the branches. That is an essential picture for the intercessor. <u>There is nothing an intercessor can accomplish apart from the Vine.</u> Perhaps God will prune away a thought that you need not pray or an action you should not do and redirect your intercession. That's okay. We are encouraged to dwell in Him and to let His Word remain in our hearts. Then we will have confidence when we pray, for our words will be in line with the will of the Father. Jesus promises us, *"If you live in Me (abide vitally united to Me) and My words remain in you and continue to live in your hearts, <u>ask whatever you will</u>, and it shall be done for you." John 15:7*

10. Have you ever noticed a pruning or a shift in how you intercede?

_____

_____

Explain a time when you had the confidence of knowing that your words were coming straight from the heart of God?

_____

_____

_____

Psalm 1:1-3 describes a person as being blessed and happy when they don't listen to ungodly counsel but to truth. I think this could include not listening to our own negative self-talk or "stinking thinking." *"But his delight and desire are in the law of the Lord, and on His law (the precepts, the instructions, the teachings of God) <u>he habitually meditates</u> (ponders and studies) by day and by night. And he shall be like a tree firmly planted (and tended) by the streams of water, <u>ready to bring forth its fruit</u> in its season; its leaf also shall not fade or wither; and everything he does shall prosper (and come to maturity)."* So again, our renewed mind is the key to our fruitfulness.

Never forget that we have seeds of life and hope already in us. (See *Galatians 5:22-23*.) <u>We can sow seeds of love or joy wherever we are.</u> The challenge is to let all the fruit of the Spirit grow and flourish in our hearts by routine "gardening." Weeds can easily take root, so we need to deal with them promptly. We also must faithfully apply the water and fertilizer of the Truth on a regular basis. The Spirit's fruit grows and matures throughout our lifetimes, but it does require our care.

Remember the encouragement in ***John 15:16*** that God Himself plants us so that we can bear fruit? Once our lives are in God's hands, He will faithfully plant us where He chooses and we get to learn how to "bloom where we are planted" and to know that our lives there will bring Him glory.

I'm also encouraged that God is always aware of where I am planted. Remember that God has chosen *you* to be planted in *a certain* field for a *certain* time to fulfill the *certain* purposes that only He knows in fullness. ***(John 15:16)*** Moreover, God longs to see the fruit of His Spirit manifested in these places throughout your whole life. I also find it interesting that He follows this verse with a clear commandment. Jesus says, ***"This is what I command you: that you love one another." John 15:17.*** Love is the principle fruit God longs to see.

In closing, let me share what one intercessor named Cheryl mentioned during a prayer meeting many years back. We were strategizing good things to do when with tears in her eyes, she said something like this, "But it's all about love. If we don't have love, we have nothing." And I would add that God is always willing to give us His love and compassion for the people we are interceding for. Ask Him and expect to see that love grow within you. We will discuss more about God's love in later chapters. After all, God is love, that's Who He is. ***(First John 4:8)***

11. What fruit of the Spirit do you most often bear in your current field?

_____

_____

_____

_____

How have you found it necessary to "weed" the garden of your heart?

_____

_____

_____

_____

How might you "water" the good seed planted in your heart?

_____

_____

_____

_____

Chapter 4:
The Way of the Cross

"Knowing the Power of the Gospel"

God uses everything, even stolen things...

Most of us can see how God has used everything so far in our lives to help us grow and mature as Christians. We also know that we have an enemy who strategizes how to steal, kill, and destroy, but his efforts don't have to end in success. In fact, Jesus came to give us an abundant and fruitful life, so He is able to override every plan of the enemy. ***John 10:10*** says ***"<u>The thief comes only in order to steal and kill and destroy</u>. I came that they may have and enjoy life, and have it in abundance (to the full, till it overflows).*** Even after all the betrayal, struggles and apparent defeats Joseph lived through, God was able to bring him into a place of victory. At the end of his story, Joseph assures his brothers, ***"As for you, you thought evil against me, but <u>God meant it for good</u>." Genesis 50:20.*** Nothing can happen in life that God is not able to redeem and turn into something good.

Many years ago, I was joining a sister intercessor in Tijuana, Mexico. I was feeling a burden for the border that divided our two countries and how it must grieve God to see a land and a people split in two because of war and politics. After some good times of intercession and divine connections, we went inside someone's home for a brief time of prayer. But when I returned to our locked car, I was surprised and disheartened to see that my backpack with camera and personal items had been stolen. Although the monetary and sentimental loss was not huge, it really bothered me.

I began the self-accusations thinking, "How could I be so stupid. I knew better than to leave any valuables in a car at night." But a few days later, on the flight back to Seattle, God revealed a "secret" to me.

<u>Nothing is ever stolen from us that God cannot redeem</u>. I saw cords extending from God's heart to me, to my backpack, and then to the person or persons who stole it. I felt there was a <u>strong magnetic pull from Father God's heart to those persons</u> because of my connection to both. *That magnetic pull was the powerful love of God.* God was showing me that what I "lost" was now being used as a point of contact or connection, enabling God's love to reach people who needed His saving grace. That one incident brought me into a deeper understanding of what intercession means.

1. Can you think of a time when someone took something from you?

_____

What did you do?

_____

_____

How might Jesus have reacted in that situation?

_____

_____

_____

Faith sees God's proof...

We choose how to see what's happening around us. Are you looking at your life, the people and even the world around you, with eyes of fear, doubt, and worry or with <u>eyes of faith</u>? After Jesus talked about some of the trials we may go through during our lives, He posed an interesting question. **Luke 18:7-8 "And will not (our just) <u>God defend and protect and avenge His elect</u> (His chosen ones), who cry to Him day and night? Will He defer then and delay help on their behalf? I tell you, He will defend and protect and avenge them speedily. However, when the Son of Man comes, <u>will He find (persistence in) faith</u> on the earth?"** Faith will be discussed more in other chapters, but I want us to be aware right away of its important role in our intercession.

Hebrews 11:1 explains what faith is. **"Now faith is the assurance (the confirmation, the title deed) of the things (we) hope for, being <u>the proof of things (we do not see</u> and the conviction of their reality (faith perceiving as real fact what is not revealed to the senses.)** According to this, living by faith actually means living with *proof* of God's reality, which may look different from the daily circumstances we face each day. All our lives, we are given the opportunity to choose which "reality" we live in, to be earthly minded or to see as God does even though it's not yet revealed to our senses.

2. What is faith to you and what part does it play in your intercession?

_____

_____

What do you do if you feel your faith is weak or shaken?

_____

_____

Highlight, click, and drag...

God once gave me a practical picture of how intercession works. Have you ever worked with a computer where you can highlight an object, click on it, and drag it to another area of your screen? At the time my backpack was stolen, I was learning to do this on my Mac computer, and I was amazed at how easily my whole screen could change.

Then I saw the spiritual application. There are two realms, two kingdoms: the kingdom of darkness (or the natural) and the kingdom of light (or God's supernatural). In between these two stands a giant cross, representing our Lord's sacrifice as our Redeemer. Our privilege as intercessors is to take people and situations in the natural realm, to focus attention on them ("highlighting" them in prayer), then to submit them into God's hands (the "click") and finally to bring them in faith to the Redeemer's cross (the "drag").

> **My hope with this study is that your eyes will be opened to see the power of the cross in your daily life and how it bridges the gap between the natural realm and the Kingdom of God.**

When we "highlight, click, and drag" to the cross, we are connecting the people or things our lives touch to the saving power of God through the cross and ultimately to His unconditional love. When and how God completes the Redemption (buying back) of these is not our responsibility. Our part is to see the need, to bring it to the cross in faith, and to release it into God's powerful hands. Maybe more than once...but all the while with faith and thanksgiving.

Philippians 4:6 says ***"Do not fret or have any anxiety about anything, but in every circumstance and in everything by prayer and petition (definite requests), with thanksgiving, continue to make your wants known to God."*** Before this verse, we are encouraged to rejoice in the Lord always; after that verse, we are assured that doing this will bring us into God's peace. ***Verse 7*** is a wonderful promise: ***"And God's peace (shall be yours, that tranquil state a soul assured of its salvation through Christ, and so fearing nothing from God and being content with its earthly lot of what-ever sort, that is, that peace) which transcends all understanding shall garrison and mount guard over your hearts and minds in Christ Jesus."***

3. Think of a person now who is in the realm of darkness (or the "natural"), try to pray for him or her by seeing that person brought to the cross and connected to God's love. See this with eyes of faith, confess it, and thank God for all He does.

   Who is that person?_____

What might God want you to know to encourage you in your prayers?

_____

_____

_____

Healing divisions...

God has recently been expanding my picture of intercession. Now instead of only seeing the <u>kingdom of darkness and the kingdom of light with the cross bridging the gaps</u>, I see <u>two different groups of people that are divided</u>. It could be two people with uncomfortable differences (like in a family) or two larger people groups (like liberals and conservatives and different denominations or religions). The size on each side of the cross doesn't matter; the principle remains the same. <u>God hates division,</u> just as He hates divorce, and His will is to make one out of the two, by bridging the gap of differences with His cross.

For Him to bridge the gap of differences, <u>each side must come to the cross, let go of their thinking that they are *right* and the other is *wrong*</u>. With an <u>attitude of surrender,</u> dying to ourselves (our own perceptions and opinions), there is hope. As long as those on each side are determined to convince the other side and turn them to their way of thinking, nothing will change. The division will only grow. This is a heart matter, of course, and our actions should continue to be according to our values. Compromise of values is not good, but negotiations are desirable when possible. Clearly hateful attacks on those who differ from us are never helpful, nor are they God's way. Both sides would benefit by <u>focusing on what they have in common</u> far more than on what divides them.

This morning I was reminded of Joshua before he conquered Jericho. An angel appeared before him, so Joshua asked, "Are you on our side or theirs?" Oddly, the angel didn't take his side even though God had already given Joshua battle plans for Jericho. The angel instead replied, ***"Neither...but as commander of the army of the Lord, I have come." Joshua 5:14.*** I think this is what God wants us to remember as we face division. Even when we think we are in the "right" during an argument, we are to surrender to God's will and to bring both sides to the cross of Jesus, in order to see all God's plans and purposes come to pass. We naturally assume God is against our enemies (those with different ways or opinions), but God's ways and thoughts are so much higher than ours. ***(Isaiah 55:8 "For My thoughts are not your thoughts, neither are your ways My ways, says the Lord.")*** Could that be why Jesus says to pray for our enemies? We probably need to hear from Him *how* to pray for them, so let's look at our hearts for the answer.

Here is an example of how intercession might become a regular part of your life. Watching the news nowadays can upset anyone with fear, frustration or worry. It's usually a good idea to limit your time with this and even to use it as an opportunity to intercede (instead of complain). That is, instead of allowing yourself to experience negative thoughts and feelings, <u>try looking at things from God's perspective</u>. Step away from your point of view and bring each side of the issues to the cross of Jesus. Release the problems and divisions you hear into the Father's hands of love. Then believe for the blood of Jesus and the power of His cross to be enough to bring unity.

Let us consider marriage or a close relationship where two people have little peace because of their differences. When both parties insist they are in the "right," division will remain. Each side should search their heart and be willing to nail all thoughts and feelings to the cross. If both parties are believers and willing to go to any lengths to see God's peace in the relationship, a wonderful verse to hold onto daily and to confess regularly is ***Ephesians 2:14: "For He is (Himself) our peace (our bond of unity and harmony). He has made us both (Jew and Gentile) one (body), and <u>has broken down (destroyed, abolished) the hostile dividing wall between us</u>, by abolishing in His (own crucified) flesh the enmity (caused by) the Law with its decrees and ordinances (which He annulled); that He from the <u>two might create in Himself one new man</u> (one new quality of humanity out of the two), so making peace."***

One actual meaning for <u>intercession is intersection</u>. Christ's cross stands vertically to intersect with mankind, just like two roads intersect. What I see as I read the verse above is the giant cross of Jesus, with one arm of the cross extended to one person, with the other arm extended to the other, and with the vertical bar of the cross representing God's love for the world. <u>With the cross between us, the saving grace of God is free to flow and to soften our hearts and bring forth change</u>.

However, if only one party is a believer (or willing to surrender his own thinking or ways), it is an act of intercession to daily bring the other person and yourself to the cross; remember it is the power of Christ's cross that can transform the hearts of men. During such times, we need to press in more than ever to our High Priest and to His throne of grace. It's only by God's grace, as we receive it and extend it to another person (forgiving their sins and overlooking our differences), that we can endure such trying times.

4. Describe a time when you were in conflict with another person, when your differences made a chasm between you.

    _____

    _____

    What did you do to resolve your differences, or were you not able to bring resolution?

    _____

    _____

What are the positive and negative effects of social media in causing peace or division?

_____

_____

The work of the cross...

Recently the whole world began reeling from the sudden outbreak of the COVID 19 corona virus. Starting in China, this new and mysterious virus has already resulted in thousands of deaths worldwide. Here in the United States, we began taking measures I've never seen taken. Our whole society shut down, resulting in financial disaster. "Social distancing and self-quarantining" became new terms for most of us, not to mention the everyday use of masks. As events were cancelled and restaurants closed, we began facing new issues. How have we as a society been responding? Multitudes began panicking, full of fear and dread; others almost ignored the warnings. This crisis, as all crises, has revealed what was in our hearts. At first, as some people rushed to hoard all they could, emptying supermarket shelves of the last roll of toilet paper and bottle of sanitizer, it became a good time to check our thoughts. Even when life is not comfortable, are we able to keep our peace and to abide in faith? What can we, as intercessors, do to help this situation? Pray, of course, and reach out to others with words and acts of love and care. But let's consider more the work of the cross and how God might want to intervene.

Never has there been a time when the **United** States of America has been so divided. For decades now the division has been growing. Currently it's so bad that many have given up believing that we could ever be united again. However, God has raised up multitudes of intercessors and prophetic voices that believe differently. The people on the left of the political aisle oppose almost anything that those on the right side of the aisle say or do and visa versa. The division in this country (and in many places around the world) is so severe, it cannot be understood with human reasoning. We are in a huge spiritual battle, for the soul of this nation and the lives of many throughout the earth. We all have heard that a house divided cannot stand, but perhaps, in addition to our intercession for our country's unity, we should pray also that Satan's "house" should also be divided. *Mark 3:25-26* states: *"And if a house is divided (split into factions and rebelling) against itself, that house will not be able to last. And if Satan has raised an insurrection against himself and is divided, he cannot stand but is (surely) coming to an end."*

I won't dwell on this much longer because it would take an entire book to explain. But let me just say that God loves America, and He will allow us to go through whatever is needed to save it. When people begin to let go of their "own way" and to surrender to Almighty God, there can be healing. Many of us have been praying *II Chronicles 7:14 (If My people who are called by my name, will humble themselves and pray and seek My face and turn from their wicked ways, then I will hear from heaven and I will heal their land.)* for decades, and God has been hearing our prayers. He is looking at the hearts of all His people, waiting for us to turn to Him and to bring ourselves to the powerful cross of Jesus that He might pour out His Spirit and bring healing. God's attention is on His people who believe; He's waiting for us to see the world from His perspective and to intercede as He leads. *I Peter 4:17-18 "For the time (has arrived) for judgment to begin with the household of God; and if it begins with us, what will (be) the end of those who do not respect or believe or obey the good news (the Gospel) of God? And if the righteous are barely saved, what will become of the godless and wicked?"*

Personally I believe God is using the current worldwide pandemic, as well as great civil unrest, to get our attention, to get us out of our own thinking and to surrender to God's thoughts and ways. That is not to say God caused horrible situations as a means of judgment, but rather that He uses ALL things, even this, to bring about His will. Many prophetic voices are declaring that a Great Awakening is about to come to the earth.

Indeed we may soon see the days prophesied in *Joel chapter 2*, where God will pour out His Spirit on all flesh. Could it be that today's tumult will usher in the glory of God? *Joel 2:28 "And afterward I will pour out My Spirit upon all flesh; and your sons and your daughters shall prophesy, your old men shall dream dreams, your young men shall see visions."* It would not surprise me at all if, once again, what the enemy means for evil, God turns into good for I believe *Habakkuk 2:14* is near at hand. *"But (the time is coming when) the earth shall be filled with the knowledge of the glory of the Lord as the waters cover the sea."* This is not too much to suffer if it will bring multitudes to know Who God is and that He is love.

5. In light of what was just written, what hope is there for this country?

   _____

   _____

   What part might you play in releasing the Holy Spirit into places of division?

   _____

   _____

   _____

The role of suffering...

The book of Hebrews gives us some vivid glimpses of Jesus as our Intercessor. And similarly it sheds light on what we are becoming as we are transformed more and more into His likeness. *Hebrews 5:7-10* describes times of passionate intercession that Jesus had while on the earth. The entire passage is good to ponder, but I'd like to focus right now on *verse 8: "Although He was a Son, He learned (active, special) obedience through what He suffered."* If the Son of God Himself had to suffer in order to learn total obedience, it shouldn't surprise us for a minute when we have hard trials. What God is looking at is <u>how we are responding to our trials.</u> Are we growing through them and becoming overcomers?

In times of suffering, I've found great comfort in knowing that God is using these hard times for my good. There is a wonderful promise in *I Peter 5:10: "And <u>after you have suffered</u> a little while, the God of all grace (Who imparts all blessing and favor), Who has called you to His (own) eternal glory in Christ Jesus, <u>will Himself complete and make you</u> what you ought to be, establish and ground you securely, and strengthen, and settle you."*

6. Think of a time when you felt you were suffering according to the will of God, that is, not because of the consequences of sin, but because God was transforming you more into His Son's image.

   Describe that time

   _____

   _____

   What was the hardest part about it?

   _____

   _____

   How did God sustain you during the suffering?

   _____

   What inner character qualities were developed in you because of what you suffered?

   _____

   _____

Whether in marriage or just everyday life, I have found that one of the most challenging, inspiring, and energizing verses in the Bible is *Galations 2:20: "I have been crucified with Christ (I Him I have shared His crucifixion); <u>it is no longer I who live</u>, but Christ (the Messiah) lives in me; and the life I now live in the body <u>I live by faith</u> in (by adherence to and reliance on and complete trust in) the son of God, Who loved me and gave Himself up for me."* When our Savior Himself said to His disciples that <u>they must take up the cross daily and follow Him</u>, He concluded that unless they do so, they are not worthy of Him. Why do we sometimes expect great things from God when we overlook what His cross should mean to us daily? Consider ***Matthew 10:38-39: "And he who <u>does</u> <u>not take up his cross</u> and follow Me (cleave steadfastly to Me, conforming wholly to My example in living and, if need be, in dying also) <u>is not worthy of Me</u>. Whoever finds his (lower) life will lose it (the higher life), and whoever loses his (lower) life on My account <u>will find it (the higher life)</u>."***

7. Based on these profound verses, how should you live each day? Describe a typical day briefly, mentioning 2-3 typical situations where you should reckon yourself "crucified with Christ."

    _____

    _____

    _____

Remember, however, that putting the cross in all things is a habit that needs to be developed. Old habits and reactions will need to be replaced over and over again until a new habit is formed. It Is said that it takes twenty one days to transform a negative belief into a healthy one and three times that (63 days) at least of <u>dedicated effort to form a new life-driven habit;</u> so hang in there, this process may take awhile.

After crucifixion comes resurrection...

I'll never forget the declaration of one of God's servants many years ago, "It's Friday, but SUNDAY'S COMING!" That is clearly the hope of Easter and the promise of victory after loss.

<u>What happens inside us once we've endured suffering in a certain area</u>? No one can deny that the Apostle Paul suffered perhaps more than any other follower. In the following passage, he talks about his desire to share in Jesus' sufferings and even death. According to this passage in ***Philippians***, we may attain a "resurrection" because of what we've endured. ***Philippians 3:10-11 "(For my determined purpose is) that I may know Him (that I may progressively become more deeply and intimately acquainted with Him...and that I may in that same way come to <u>know the power</u> <u>outflowing from His resurrection</u>...and that I may so <u>share His sufferings</u> as to be continually transformed (in spirit into His likeness even) to His death (in the hope) that if possible <u>I may</u> <u>attain to the (spiritual and moral)resurrection</u> (that lifts me) out from among the dead (even while in the body.)*** <u>If we are crucified with Christ, we will also experience the power of His resurrection</u> during our lifetime on this earth. In fact, anything that experiences the cross of Jesus will experience new life. That's why we are to bring people to the cross in our prayers.

8. What do you think Paul was explaining in these verses?

    _____

    _____

What would resurrection look like in your everyday life?

_____

_____

The **sixth chapter of Romans** explains how we can have resurrection power and true victory in our lives. It involves dying to ourselves so that His life might be seen in us. **Romans 6:4-5 explains: "We were buried therefore with Him by the <u>baptism into death</u>, so that just as Christ was raised from the dead by the glorious (power) of the Father, so we too might (habitually) live and behave in newness of life. For if we have become one with Him by sharing a death like His, we shall also be (one with Him in <u>sharing) His resurrection</u> (by a new life lived for God)."**

So we can expect newness of life and peace to come in every area where we have crucified our flesh. Remember that <u>we are choosing each moment of each day</u> to live in our flesh (our natural thinking) or in the Spirit (God's way of thinking) according to **Romans 8:5-6.**

We learn to experience the Spirit-led life as we grow. <u>We become willing to give up our near-sighted, self-centered thinking/acting, surrendering ourselves by taking up the cross daily.</u> **Verse 7** makes the clear explanation: **"(That is) because the <u>mind of the flesh</u> (with its carnal thoughts and purposes) is hostile to God, for it <u>does not submit itself to God's Law</u>; indeed it cannot."**

9. What, then, does it mean to you, in your daily life or intercession, when you've crucified your flesh and experienced the resurrection life of Christ?

_____

_____

_____

Resurrection includes compassion and authority...

Let's explore resurrection power a little further. Let's say we are interceding for a loved one who is facing a terrible disease. As we allow our <u>natural thinking and feelings to be crucified</u> with Christ, we know we are connecting with the only One who can save, heal, and restore. We are connecting with the only One who knows the Father's will for that person. Then *after crucifixion must come resurrection.* So whatever the outcome of our intercession, we can <u>know</u> it is to God's glory and according to the Father's will.

Now ponder more what happened to our Lord after His resurrection. Could His enemies still taunt Him? Could any earthly power control Him? Where was He to be seated? At the right hand of His

Father, the Almighty God, right? From that position, Jesus began His rule as King of Kings and also as our High Priest and Intercessor. ***Philippians 2: 8-10 "And after He had appeared in human form, <u>He abased and humbled Himself</u> (still further) and carried His obedience to the extreme of death, even the death of the cross! Therefore (because He stooped so low) God has highly exalted Him and has freely <u>bestowed on Him the name that is above every name,</u> that in (at) the name of Jesus every knee should (must) bow, in heaven and on earth and under the earth."***

In every area where we suffer and allow ourselves to surrender to God's perfect will, we emerge victorious and with a new or deeper Christ-likeness. <u>More of Christ's compassion and authority are imparted to us.</u> For example, if we are inflicted with a disease or beside a loved one who is suffering, don't <u>we develop a passionate empathy</u> for others going through a similar situation? Doesn't our heart quite naturally <u>connect to the Father's heart and thereby come closer to experiencing His love and authority</u> in that situation? It is because of our suffering, then, that we can now intercede more effectively and minister better to others in similar situations. The question is: Are we becoming *bitter* or *better* through our suffering?

Even further, Christ's resurrection means He began ruling with supreme authority and power. Could that mean that God allows us to experience certain sufferings so that He might give us <u>specific Christ-like authority and power</u> in every area where we experience His crucifixion and His resurrection? Consider this passage in ***Colossians 2:10: "And you are in Him, made full and having come to fullness of life (<u>in Christ you too are filled with the God-head</u>—Father, Son, and Holy Spirit—and reach full spiritual stature). And <u>He is the Head of all rule and authority (of every angelic principality and power)."</u>***

10. Have you interceded for others in a situation you experienced yourself?

_____

_____

Explain when you have suffered in an area that has resulted in great empathy for others in that situation.

_____

_____

Did you feel greater authority as you prayed?

_____

_____

From the cost of the cross comes the power of the Gospel...

As we conclude these thoughts on the cross of Jesus and what it means in our daily lives, let me emphasize one last essential point.

The reason why there is such power in the cross is one hundred percent because of the incredibly precious blood that was shed there for our sakes. <u>It was shed because of love</u>, because the Almighty God so loved us who were born into sin that He would give us that which was dearest to Him, His only begotten son, indeed a very part of Himself. *(John 3:16 says "For God so greatly loved and deeply prized the world that He even gave up His only begotten Son...")*

To live victorious lives, to intercede effectively, we must always keep in mind the cost of True Love. It cost the Father a great deal to send forth His Beloved Son into a hateful and cruel world where He knew He would be despised, rejected, and crucified. The cost was huge.

What is the cost of effective intercession? God is waiting for nothing less than a <u>totally surrendered vessel through which He can pour His glory</u>. That's the type of Person He was looking at when He watched His Son pay the price. Does He expect less from us as we become co-intercessors with the great High Priest? Let us remember that Jesus wasn't probably just referring to physical death when He said, ***"No one has greater love (no one has shown stronger affection) than to <u>lay down (give up) his own life for his friends</u>," John 15:13.***

11. What specifically is the price God is asking you to pay as you intercede with the love of God? (i.e. Are there thoughts you must crucify, things you must surrender?)

_____

_____

_____

_____

Because Jesus paid the ultimate price, we can put ourselves and those we intercede for under the blood of the Lamb. It's really quite easy. Simply <u>surrender, believe and declare.</u> What happens next is that <u>God's powerful, life-changing grace is released upon us and those we intercede for</u>.

Our part is to surrender ourselves, to take up His cross daily, and to die to our flesh. God's part is to bring forth life and resurrection power in our daily lives while we're still on earth. That's the power of the Gospel and the incredible work of God's grace.

Chapter 5:
The Journey to Know Love

"Building Life on a Sure Foundation"

The only secure foundation...

When we begin our Christian lives, the Holy Spirit takes up residence in our spirits. *I Corinthians 6:19 says "Do you not know that <u>your body is the temple</u> (the very sanctuary) of the Holy Spirit Who lives within you, Who you have received (as a Gift) from God? <u>You are not your own.</u> "*

Another way to think of this born-again experience is that <u>God plants the seed of His love in our hearts.</u> The Christian life, then, is learning how to nourish that seed and to let it grow in our hearts. As we allow parts of our natural soul-life (thoughts, emotions, and our will) to surrender to the work of the cross (as explained in the last chapters) the plant of God's love takes root, blooms and produces fruit.

Let's consider another metaphor to understand how God's love grows in our lives. It can be compared to the construction of a house. *Hebrews 3:4 says "For (of course) every house is built and furnished by someone, but the <u>Builder of all things and the Furnisher</u> (of the entire equipment of all things) is God."* Once again, the Bible compares our bodies to an eternal house, in *II Corinthians 5:1 "For we know that if the tent which is our earthly home is destroyed (dissolved) we have from God a building, a house not made with hands, eternal in the heavens."* Both of these verses emphasize that God is the Builder of our lives, but as we are seeing, we can either help or hinder His work in us.

When a house is to be built, the ground must first be excavated. This includes removing boulders, trees, and dirt in order to prepare the land for the pouring of a foundation. This could be compared to what God does in our hearts before we are saved to get us ready to receive His Spirit. Once the land is ready, the foundation is poured. If you have ever purchased a house, you know how important it is to have a secure foundation. *Matthew 7:24* talks about the wise one who builds his house upon the rock so that it can withstand all the elements of life. Jesus, of course is the Rock, as well as the chief Cornerstone *(Ephesians 2:20).* Once we begin our Christian life, we do well to remember that the foundation of our eternal life is Jesus Himself, the embodiment of God Who is Love.

TOUCHING THE HEART OF GOD

1. Was there a time in your life (before you became a Christian) when you felt the Lord may have been "excavating" your heart in preparation for receiving His Spirit?

_____

_____

Have you come to recognize that the entire foundation for your Christian life is the Love of God? What does that imply?

_____

_____

My hope for you, as you thoughtfully reflect on the verses in this chapter, is that you will see how God's love has always been there for you and that it is the very sure foundation of your whole life.

Building God's house in you...

Once the foundation for a house is solid, the workers begin to frame, to rough-in rooms, and to cover the whole structure with a roof. Once this is done, the dry wall and painting are completed. Last are added the flooring, appliances, and finally furnishings and decorations. We could probably look back on our lives and see different stages where our spiritual houses were being completed. And since God has been the Builder, we have wonderfully built houses. *"Come and, like living stones, be yourselves <u>built into a spiritual house</u>, for a holy (dedicated, consecrated) priesthood, to offer up those spiritual sacrifices that are acceptable and pleasing to God through Jesus Christ. For thus it stands in Scripture: Behold, I am laying in Zion a <u>chosen (honored), precious chief Cornerstone</u>, and he who believes in Him (who adheres to, trusts in, and relies on Him) shall <u>never be disappointed or put to shame</u>." I Peter 2:5 -6*

We have some powerful promises for our spiritual houses. *"Through skillful and godly <u>Wisdom is a house (a life, a home, a family) built, and by understanding it is established</u> (on a sound and good foundation.)" Proverbs 24:3.* And *Isaiah 60:18 "<u>Violence shall no more be heard in your land,</u> nor devastation or destruction within your borders, but you shall call your walls Salvation and your gates Praise."*

Nevertheless, although God's love is the foundation of our house, we choose if we let him complete our house or if we frustrate His plans. The passage from *I Corinthians 3, verses 7-17* talks about the house of our lives and how what is worthy will last. *Verses 12- 13* explain *"But if anyone builds upon the Foundation, whether it be with <u>gold, silver, precious stones, wood, hay, straw</u>, the work* *of each (one will become (plainly, openly) known (shown for what it is); for the day (of Christ) will disclose and declare it, because it will be revealed with fire, and the fire will test and critically appraise the character and worth of the work each person has done."* In other words, when we face Jesus some day, all we do in our lives that is made of wood, hay, and straw (or by our flesh rather than by His Spirit) will be burned. Only the precious works of the Spirit (gold, silver, precious stones)will last. ***Verse 15*** explains what happens to the lives we build*: "But if any person's work is burned up (under the test), he will <u>suffer the loss (of it all, losing his reward)</u>, though he himself will be saved, but only as (one who has passed) through fire."* Once our lives are built on the foundation of God's love, they will be saved; however, God tests us throughout our lives, so that we may be purified and someday rewarded for all the precious gems our lives have created.

God knows our hearts, even as He knew Job's heart and that Job's house would be well built. ***Job 23:10 "But He knows the way that I take (He has concern for it, appreciates and pay attention to it). <u>When He has tried me, I shall come forth as refined gold</u> (pure and luminous)."*** So be encouraged that God is on your side, and He will be faithful to complete each life that has a foundation of His love.

2. What's the most encouraging promise you hold onto while your house is being built?

___

___

___

Is there a trial you have endured that you feel may someday bring you an eternal reward?

___

___

___

Understanding the foundation of Love...

Since God is Love ***(I John 4:8)*** <u>and His Love is perfect and unconditional</u>, we can be encouraged that He will never love us more than He does today (no matter how well we behave) nor will His love ever be less even when we stumble. To successfully walk in the power of God's love, we first must understand it and recognize that it is the foundation of our Christian lives. To do this, let's look at ***First Corinthians 13.***

In ***verses one, two and three***, the Apostle Paul explains that nothing we do has much value unless it comes from a heart of love. Then beginning with ***verse four until verse eight***, he describes what we are like if we live in love. Remember as you read these qualities that this <u>describes God's heart of love for *you* as well as a description of how we are encouraged to build our lives.</u>

Verse 4: "<u>*Love endures long and is patient and kind*</u>; *love <u>never is envious nor boils over with jealousy,</u> is <u>not boastful</u> or vainglorious, does not display itself haughtily.*" So right now, honestly evaluate yourself as to how well that describes your daily interactions at home or elsewhere.

3. How have you learned to be patient and kind?

_____

_____

_____

What do you do when you begin to feel jealous of a friend or co-worker?

_____

_____

_____

Verse 5: "*It is <u>not conceited</u> (arrogant and inflated with pride); it is <u>not rude</u> (unmannerly) and does not act unbecomingly. Love (God's love in us) does <u>not insist on its own rights</u> or its own way, for it is <u>not self-seeking</u>; it is <u>not touchy or fretful or resentful</u>); it <u>takes no account of the evil</u> done to it (it pays no attention to a suffered wrong)*."

4. This is a great reminder to surrender our "rightness" in conversations. Is there a time when you surrendered your "self-seeking" to preserve a relationship?

_____

_____

Are you easily offended or have you learned to let go of the everyday offenses of others?

_____

_____

Verse 6: "*It <u>does not rejoice at injustice and unrighteousness,</u> but rejoices when right and truth prevail.*" Verse 7: Love <u>bears up under anything</u> and everything that comes, is ever <u>ready to</u>

believe the best of every person; its hopes are fadeless under all circumstances, and it endures everything (without weakening). Verse 8: Love never fails (never fades out or becomes obsolete of comes to an end.) This is how God considers *you*! How He loves to see you discover truth. He never gives up on you, but believes the best of you even when you fall short. His hopes for you never fail or even fade. <u>When we finally realize how great is His love for us, we can begin to show this same kind of love</u> to others. It may be true that we cannot love others until we first love ourselves. The chapter ends with *verse 13: And so faith, hope, love abide...these three; but the greatest of these is love.*

5. Have you ever felt God was giving up on you or someone you love? How do these verses say otherwise?

_____

_____

_____

Is there a person or situation that you feel you cannot endure? How might knowing God's love in you make a huge difference?

_____

_____

The journey to know perfect love...

I remember when I was saved as a child by hearing *John 3:16*: *"For God <u>so loved</u> the world that He gave His only begotten Son, that whosoever believeth in Him should not perish but have everlasting life."* My child-like faith told me I would go to heaven when I died because I believed in Him. What a relief that was to me! I did not realize that at that moment, when I knew so little about the Lord, He had entered into a covenant relationship with <u>me</u>, just a little child.

Soon after, I heard the verse about loving the Lord with all your heart, soul, and mind *(Matthew 22:37)*, and I thought, "I believe in Jesus, but I don't love Him. How can you love someone you don't see?" I believe the Almighty God looked down on my young heart and heard that unspoken question. I believe that was when I began on <u>my life-long journey of knowing God's love for me and growing in love for Him.</u> Now looking back I see that *we love Him because He first loved us. (I John 4:19)* As we go through life's challenges, He demonstrates His faithfulness, and we begin to see how His Love is the sure foundation of our lives.

I began to understand this early in my adult Christian walk when I was plagued with irrational fears for my health. No matter how I tried to quiet my mind and reassure myself that I was just over-reacting to the symptoms of stress that were manifesting in my body, <u>I could not let go of this fear</u>. One night, feeling especially fearful, but also fed up with feeling that way, I knelt before the Lord in prayer. I saw myself taking that fear off me and nailing it to the cross of Jesus. I repented of my fear and asked God to free me from its control. It was a short prayer, and I didn't feel great relief when I was done. However, as I went back to bed and reached to turn off my bedside light, I heard a faint chuckle followed by the words, "<u>Don't you know how much I love you</u>?" I thought to myself, "I guess not," and went to sleep not realizing I had just heard the still small voice of God,

The next day, however, I was listening to a Christian teaching on the radio when I heard the verse in ***I John, "<u>Perfect love casts out fear</u>."*** Then I understood in an instant that I had heard God's voice gently telling me that the key to overcoming fear was LOVE. Only the power of love can set us free from fear's ugly grip. ***"There is no fear in love (dread does not exist), but full-grown (complete, <u>perfect) love turns fear out of doors</u> and expels every trace of terror! For fear brings with it the thought of punishment, and (so) <u>he who is afraid has not reached the full maturity of love (is not yet grown into love's complete perfection)</u>." I John 4:18***

And so it was that I set out on my journey to know love. God was saying to my heart, "Now I will begin to show you what true love is all about."

6. Can you recall a time in your life when God first showed you about His love for you? If so, please summarize that time. If not, why not ask God to show you more of his love?

_____

_____

_____

_____

Do you have a favorite verse that God has given to show you His love?

_____

_____

_____

_____

The call to intimacy...

On my journey to know the love of God, I hoped God would bring me a godly husband who would lay down his own self-life for me and love me as Christ loved the church. And although this seemed to be true for a season, my marriage soon became an experience of great disappointment and disillusionment. My earthly covenant of love was broken.

My husband had his own issues that God was dealing with, but God had another love-plan for me. He wanted to draw me only to Himself, for me to come to know Him as my Provider Father, as my faithful Husband, and as my ever-present Counselor and Friend. I knew this was the love-call of the ***Song of Solomon*** and a time to come away with Him and to know Him in a new and deeper way. I treasure those days and His words: ***"My beloved speaks and says to me, <u>'Rise up, my love, my fair one, and come away</u>. For, behold, the winter is past; the rain is over and gone. The flowers appear on the earth; the time of the singing of birds) has come, and the voice of the turtledove is heard in our land.'" Song of Solomon 2:10-12.***

I remember asking God what intimacy with Him would look like. What I learned was that it is the pouring out of two hearts. I would pour out my heart to God and then He would pour out His heart to fill me up. Wow, I thought that made sense. Then I felt God gently remind me, "but you rarely sit still long enough to let me fill you up."

Although I responded to His call to know Him more intimately, I had much more to learn on my journey into intimacy. I learned that this process takes time and life experiences. The passage in ***Ephesians 3:16-19*** became my life testimony and my prayer for family members: ***"May He grant you out of the rich <u>treasury of His glory</u> to be strengthened and reinforced with <u>mighty power in the inner man</u> by the Holy Spirit Himself indwelling your innermost being and personality. May Christ through your faith actually dwell (settle down, abide, make His permanent home) in your hearts! <u>May you be rooted deep in love and founded securely on love.</u> That you may have the power and be strong to apprehend and grasp with all the saints (God's devoted people, the <u>experience of that love</u>) what is the breadth and length and height and depth of it; that you may really come to know (practically, through experience for yourselves) the love of Christ, <u>which far surpasses mere knowledge without experience</u>; that you may be <u>filled through all your being unto all the fullness of God</u> (may have the richest measure of the divine Presence, and become a body wholly filled and flooded with God Himself!"***

I began to understand that you don't really *know* something <u>until you experience it first-hand, until your life experiences validate it</u>. This is true of all truth; knowing it in your mind and living it out are quite different. The same is true for knowing God's love. You can know about it intellectually, but it's not until your life experiences reveal God's love in different ways, that you really begin to KNOW that love.

It takes time and many varied experiences to know God, but as Jesus prayed, ***"This is eternal life: <u>to know You</u>, the only true and real God, and (likewise) <u>to know Him</u>, Jesus Christ (the Anointed One, the Messiah), Who You have sent." (John 17:3)*** This journey of love is the journey we all are on. As I began to experience a deeper, more consistent love relationship with Jesus, <u>I began to know Him better, and to know Him enabled me to trust Him</u>. I began to understand I could trust God in the areas He had proven Himself to me, and I looked forward to knowing Him in new areas of my life.

7. In what specific ways has God demonstrated His love to you or how might you expect to see His love demonstrated *today*?

_____

_____

_____

If God doesn't show His love the way you expect, think about this truth: "God wants us to enjoy His <u>presence</u> more than His <u>presents</u>."

8. Do you think we must <u>know</u> God's love in order to <u>show</u> God's love? Explain your answer.

_____

_____

_____

_____

Securing your house from enemy attacks...

Recently I had a break-in in my home in the middle of the day while I was gone for only an hour. Although this was disturbing, little was stolen and I soon felt God's peace. I had never experienced this before, and it did motivate me to get a security system for my home. Furthermore, I recalled the promise of the Passover, where God's people applied the blood to their doorways so that the enemy would pass over them. ***Exodus 12: 21-23*** explains the first Passover and ***verse 23*** says***, "For the Lord will pass through to slay the Egyptians; and when He sees the blood upon the lintel and the two side posts, the Lord will <u>pass over the door</u> and <u>will not allow the destroyer</u> to come into your houses to slay you."*** So the best security for your home is to declare the power of Christ's blood over every door and window of your home.

Much as we are able to secure our physical homes by pleading His blood, we can also experience the power of His blood over our souls. We all have specific vulnerabilities or "buttons" that the enemy can push to cause us to lose our peace. The Lord would have us be <u>aware of which enemies attack our souls, when, and why.</u> Let's explore this a bit so that we might become experts in resisting them.

James 5:7 says "So <u>be subject to God. Resist the devil</u> (stand firm against him), and he will flee from you." Never forget that the power to resist our enemies comes from our submission to God. ***John 10:10*** reminds us that Satan comes to steal, kill, and destroy, we should pay attention to the "enemies" that rob us of the peace and joy that Jesus promises.

9. Have you ever applied the blood of Jesus to your physical home or to the spiritual house of your life? If so, explain that here or write out your confession of faith.

    _____

    _____

    _____

Even though we face enemies of our faith, we can be prepared and withstand every attack. Each enemy of our Father God that we overcome makes our foundation of love more secure. So as our hearts learn to recognize and overcome the enemy's strategies, we get stronger.

Perhaps the most common enemy we all face and must learn to conquer is *fear.* Just as our love becomes worship for God, who is Love, <u>our fear is actually worship of Satan, who is out to kill, steal, and destroy</u> (see ***John 10:10***). If we ever have a fearful thought, or a thought that causes us anxiety or worry, we can be certain that thought does not come from God. Moreover, it is a thought we are able to resist and forbid to take hold of our hearts and minds. Focus instead on God's love by remembering that God's ***"perfect love casts out fear" (I John 4:18).***

A great strategy when facing fearful thoughts is to spend more time in praise and worship. That enables us to operate in the spirit opposite of fear: love. And that's the time to reach out even more with God's love to others. ***I John 4:7-8*** reminds us ***"Beloved, <u>let us love one another</u>, for love is (springs) from God; and he who loves (his fellowmen) is begotten (born) of God and is coming (progressively) to know and understand God (to perceive and recognize and get a better and clearer knowledge of Him). He who does not love has not become acquainted with God (does not and never did know Him), for God is love.*** <u>When we focus on love instead of fear, Satan will soon give up</u> attacking us this way. Whenever we are harassed by a fear, it's a reminder to submit our minds and hearts to God and to resist that negative thought ***(James 5:7).***

If you have never read the tremendous allegory called *Hinds' Feet on High Places* by Hannah Hurnard, I would highly recommend it. It's the story of little Much-Afraid's journey to know the Love of God and to see her promised destiny fulfilled, as experienced in the high places of His Kingdom. First the Good Shepherd calls her to follow Him, and He implants the seed of His love in her heart. When she begins her journey, she is given two companions, Sorrow and Suffering, who she learns to appreciate during her journey. She suffers a series of attacks by her worst enemies: Craven Fear, Pride, Resentment, Bitterness, and Self-pity. Eventually she begins to recognize all their tactics and strategies, and she learns how to resist them. Through her travels, the Good Shepherd appears whenever she calls for Him, and in the end, she is transformed and receives a new name. It's a delightful read that causes us to look deeply at our own journeys to know God better.

10. What are the worst enemies of your soul that you face and how have you learned to recognize them quickly and to resist them?

The process of knowing God's love and peace...

Whether we are building a home or developing a relationship, we always know that the process takes time. We have the blueprints to living in God's love and to enjoying His perfect peace, but it takes time for us to know the reality of these things. God has already given us the totality of His love and His constant peace, but it takes trials and tribulations along with our surrender and trust to experience His love and peace in our everyday lives. There will be days when we can actually feel the Father's love and the peace that Jesus left us, but then there are other days. Did God change His mind or His promise?

Whenever we feel distanced from God, it's good to remember that He never moved; we must have. That's always a reminder for us to look into our own heart and mind to see what could be blocking the flow of His Spirit. I remember years ago learning that God may have different expectations for His children than He does for His more mature sons and daughters. He wants us to learn how to constantly trust the power of His love, whether we feel it or not.

God's covenant of love and peace was fully completed when Christ gave His life on the cross, but as we live, we will be growing in His grace from glory to glory. *"And all of us, as with unveiled face, (because we) continued to behold (in the Word of God) as in a mirror the glory of the Lord, are <u>constantly being transfigured into His very own image</u> in ever increasing splendor and from one degree of glory to another; (for this comes) from the Lord (Who is) the Spirit." I Corinthians 3:18*

Once again, I love all the *third chapter of Ephesians*, but *verse 19* in the Amplified Bible explains this process beautifully. *"(That you may really come) to <u>know (practically, through experience for yourselves)</u> the love of Christ, which <u>far surpasses mere knowledge (without experience)</u>; that you may be filled (through all your being) unto all the fullness of God (may have the richest measure of the divine Presence, and become a body <u>wholly filled and flooded with God Himself</u>."* Wow! That's the process of our Christian lives; that's the goal we should all aspire to; and that's why we can count it all joy when we go through tough times. (See *James chapter 1.*)

In *John 14:27 Jesus* said, *"My peace I give you"* and it's certainly not from this world. What this means to me is that when my heart is not at peace, I need to ask God why. Assuming I have not willfully sinned against Him (which obviously results in a lack of peace), I've learned to look at my thoughts and my belief system (which often come from this world). *Colossians 3:2-3 exhorts us, "And set your minds and <u>keep them set on what is above</u> (the higher things), not on the things that are on the earth. <u>For (as far as this world is concerned) you have died</u>, and your (new, real) life is hidden with Christ in God."* Our feelings are the result of our beliefs. And as many of us know, Satan's battleground for us personally is our minds. As we learn to cast down negative thoughts that oppose the perfect will of God and to bring every thought into obedience to the mind of Christ, <u>we will know God's peace and we will pray more effectively.</u>

One of my favorite promises concerning peace follows Paul's advice to not fret but make our wants known to God. *Ephesians 4:7 "And <u>God's peace</u> (shall be yours, that tranquil state of a soul assured of its salvation through Christ, and so <u>fearing nothing</u> from God and <u>being content</u> with its earthly lot of whatever sort that is, that peace) which transcends all understanding <u>shall garrison and mount guard over your heart and minds in Christ Jesus."</u>*

Just as we *"strive to enter that rest" (Hebrews 4:11)*, we struggle to regain God's peace over and over during each new trial. *But it does get easier. Through each trial, our trust and confidence in God grows and deepens.* We learn that His peace is always available, and that it's not just denying our feelings or suppressing our fears and anxieties. Neither is God's peace a standard we can achieve through our efforts. <u>Peace is a *beautiful result of God's grace* at work in us.</u> We are learning to go through whatever life brings our way with perfect peace, knowing that all that happens must first pass through our loving Father's hands and that everything is subject to God's law of love which governs or controls our life (which we will address further in the next chapter).

When life spins out of control, <u>we may be learning to know that our loving Father is still in control</u>, but we are still human. We should never feel guilty with our struggles to abide in His peace. His love totally covers our humanity. His covenant blessings are forever ours, and we can trust His faithful love. This is an unchangeable, unshakable absolute. It's good to remember that our growth and understanding will continue until the day we see Jesus face to face. ***"And after you have suffered a little while, the God of all grace (Who imparts all blessing and favor), Who has called you to His (own) eternal glory in Christ Jesus, will Himself <u>complete and make you what you ought to be</u>, establish and ground you securely, and strengthen, and settle you." I Peter 5:10***

11. Explain where you are in the process of knowing how much God loves you? Is God's love for you becoming a reality in your daily life? How might that change your perspective on suffering?

_____

_____

_____

_____

_____

_____

Embracing God's promise of love...

In reflecting back on my journey to knowing God's perfect love, I believe the "call to intimacy" was like a betrothal time for me. I began to know my Lord and to fall in love with Him. But it was a few years, with many deep lessons of love, before I think He became my Husband. First, I needed to be purified of a deep longing in my heart for natural love (which can be imperfect and disappoint), and I needed to make a determined love commitment to seek Jesus and His Kingdom above all else. There were many hard times, but they were some of my sweetest days.

I felt God was saying this to me: ***"There I will give her vineyards and make the Valley of Achor (troubling) to be for her a <u>door of hope and expectation</u>. And she shall sing there and respond as in the days of her youth and as at the time when she came up out of the land of Egypt, and it shall be in that day, says the Lord, that <u>you will call Me Ishi (my Husband)</u>, and you shall no more call Me Baali." Hosea 2:15-16***

When the time came that God's covenant of love was established in my heart, it was the time of my "marriage." I have never been the same since that time. It was the summer of 1994 and I spontaneously went on a trip to Hawaii with a girlfriend, but all the while I knew it was my honeymoon with Jesus. He's so sweet; He knew this trip was a desire of my heart. He even sealed the time with a stunning rainbow that confirmed His covenant with me. When we enter that type of relationship with Jesus, we benefit from all that His name represents.

As the years followed, even through other trials and tests, I have held onto one verse as a life-line or anchor for my soul: ***"I am by Beloved's and He is mine. The banner of His love has been established over my life." (See Song of Solomon 7:10 and 2:4.)***

Another powerful promise is ***Jeremiah 31:3 "The Lord appeared from of old to me saying, Yes, I have <u>loved you with an everlasting love</u>; therefore <u>with loving-kindness have I drawn you</u> and continued My faithfulness to you."***

For those who want steps to know the Father's love more deeply, it's as simple as 1, 2, 3: *receive it, believe it*, and live to *declare it*. However simple this sounds, it is a deep heart issue and is rarely a speedy process. In fact, we spend our entire life learning to know and trust God's heart of love for us and to love Him wholeheartedly in return. But what a rewarding journey that is!

Chapter 6:
God's Kingdom of Love

"Remembering the Law Governing Your Life"

God's law and judgment...

With Christ's sacrificial death, we who believe enter into the promises of the New Testament, the New Covenant. In order to abide in all the blessings of that covenant of love, we want to consider its foundation but also its laws and principles.

Why and how did almighty God establish a new covenant with people? Why wasn't the old covenant established with Abraham good enough? The short answer is that <u>God knows peoples' hearts, better than we ourselves do</u>, and He knew no one could live without sin or fulfill all the demands of the law. He established the law (with the ten commandments and all the other requirements of the Old Testament) to show us our need for a Savior. ***"For all have sinned and fallen short of the glory of God." (Romans 3:23)*** We all need a Savior.

If we are trying to prove our righteousness, we might as well give up now. God knows we will never measure up to that; only His sinless Son ever could. ***"But God shows and clearly proved His (own) love for us by the fact that <u>while we were still sinners, Christ (the Messiah, the Anointed One) died for us</u>." (Romans 5:8)*** That's the essence of the Gospel, the Good News. God doesn't condemn people while they live because of their sins; instead <u>He sees each person's life as worthy of redemption, able to have their sins covered with His love demonstrated through Christ's sacrifice</u>. God sees the goodness and potential in the heart of each person, and He would that all people be saved (See ***I Timothy 2:4.***)

In addition, unlike many human beings, Father God can be trusted because He never lies. ***"<u>God is not a man</u>, that He should tell or act a lie, neither the son of man, that He should feel repentance or compunction for what He has promised. Has He said and shall He not do it? Or has He spoken and shall He not make it good?" Numbers 23:19***

Why would God treat sinful mankind that way? We can't imagine because our concept of LOVE is so distorted, so arbitrary and conditional. But not God's. ***"For God loved the world (<u>all the people He created</u>, even the most wretched and unlovable)so very much, that He gave us His dearest, Son (to pay the price of pure obedience and spotless sinlessness) so that if we would only believe in***

Him, we could taste the Father's love and live with Him for all eternity." (My paraphrase of ***John 3:16)*** That's the heart of God, and it never changes. ***"Jesus Christ (the Messiah) is always the same: yesterday, today, yes and forever (to the ages)." Hebrews 13:8***

God's love for us will never be less and never be greater (no matter what we do and don't do). It's unconditional and can never be earned. It's just Who He is. That's the heart of love the Father wants to develop in all His people. Some day we will all stand before God as Judge, and perhaps He will ask each of us if we learned to love others as He did. That's why we all are on this journey to know His love, to live in it, and to give it freely to others.

Considering our judgments…

Let's look honestly a minute at our human love, so different from God's pure love, and the tendency to judge others. I'd like to first say that Christians are to judge sin and may need to help a brother or sister struggling with sin. This type of righteous judgment is explained carefully in scriptures such as in ***Matthew 18:15*** and ***I Corinthians 5:11-13*** because we must always look at the heart of others as explained in ***John 7:24: "Be honest in your judgment and do not decide at a glance (superficially and by appearances); but judge fairly and righteously."***

My focus here, however, is on the *unrighteous judgments* we make in haste or ignorance which may be formed because of our pride or self-centeredness. Paul advises all people clearly in ***Romans 12:3 "not to estimate and think of himself more highly than he ought (not to have an exaggerate opinion of his own importance), but to rate his ability with sober judgment…"***

Before we find fault with anyone, we should always search our own hearts and ask ourselves why we feel as we do. We tend to love others who seem worthy of our respect and love, never mind all the others who fall short of that. And how can we possibly love those who offend us or abuse us? That just doesn't seem right. We say we should love the sinner and hate the sin, but how do we do that? Each of us has an internal check list for those who deserve to be loved. We subconsciously judge everyone as either worthy or unworthy of our love and even of God's love. Our subjective and human criteria are very different from God's. Are we able to love those who are different from us, those who may seem despicable in our eyes (like murderers and abusers) or even those who hold other beliefs? How often do we step back from our evaluations, our judgments, and surrender our own perspective so that we might begin to see others from the Father's perspective?

I recently saw again the last hour of the movie called ***The Shack,*** (from the book by William P. Young) where Mackenzie was in the cave with Wisdom herself. This scene presents an incredibly deep revelation of the heart of God. If God loves everyone the same, does He want any of them to perish? Mackenzie was so hurt by the man who murdered his innocent daughter that he vowed never to forgive him. But Wisdom challenged him that he was to assume the role of judge and send one of his two children to heaven while sending the other one to hell. Of course, he could not do that. Neither can Almighty God judge some people worthy of salvation and condemn others to hell. And yet we sometimes <u>fail to forgive others, and our judgment locks them and ourselves into sin.</u>

In ***Matthew 7:1-5*** Jesus warns his disciples ***"<u>Do not judge and criticize</u> and condemn others, so that you may not be judged and criticized and condemned yourselves."*** He wonders how people could get upset with the speck in others' eyes while being unaware of the log in their own eyes. Believers often are very obedient in other areas while letting this critical heart attitude and negative speaking (including gossip) be part of them. Lord, wake us up to this sin. ***I Peter 4:17-18*** warns us ***"For the time (has arrived) for <u>judgment to begin with the household of God:</u> and if it begins with us, what will (be) the end of those who do not respect or believe or obey the good news (the Gospel) of God? And if the righteous are barely saved, what will become of the godless and wicked?"*** When we judge others and refuse to forgive them, there can be serious consequences. ***Matthew 18:34-35*** explains how a master's wrath turns someone who would not show mercy over to the torturers and Jesus added ***"So also My heavenly Father will deal with every one of you <u>if you do not freely forgive your brother from your heart his offenses.</u>"***

That's why <u>God hates it when we are critical and fault finding</u>, judging others unrighteously from a human standpoint. Of course, we are never to compromise the truth of what is right and wrong, good or evil. It's just that we are always to separate the sin from the sinner. <u>When we refuse to forgive an offense</u> or a person who has wronged us in any way, <u>we are violating God's type of love.</u> God's love never refuses the power of forgiveness when dealing with a person. When we surrender our opinions and judgments, we open a channel for God's love and redemption to flow though and reach peoples' hearts. ***I Timothy 2:3-4*** says ***"For such (praying) is good and right, and (it is) pleasing and acceptable to God our Savior, <u>Who wishes all men to be saved</u> and (increasingly) to perceive and recognize and discern and know precisely and correctly the (divine) Truth."*** Perhaps God's way could be simply put: *<u>love people and hate sin; learn to give and forgive freely</u>*. That no doubt is the message of Jesus' life and death on the cross.

1. Why do Christians so easily judge others? Is there anything we should judge?

    _____

    _____

    _____

    How might a loving God bring judgment to His household? ***(I Peter 4:17-18)***

    _____

    _____

    _____

The power of forgiveness...

God's way of bringing people to repentance is never by criticizing or judging them but rather by showing them kindness and mercy (although at times that includes "tough love"). *James 2:13* explains *"For to him who has shown no mercy the judgment will be merciless, but <u>mercy (full of glad confidence) exults victoriously over judgment</u>."* And *Romans 2:4b "Are you unmindful or actually ignorant of the fact that <u>God's kindness is intended to lead you to repent</u> (to change your mind and inner man to accept God's will?"*

<u>Could it be that forgiveness is the most powerful act we can do as a Christian</u>? Could forgiveness be our <u>most powerful weapon against Satan</u> himself? *"If you forgive anyone anything I too forgive that one; and what I have forgiven, if I have forgiven anything, has been for your sakes in the presence (and with the approval) of Christ the Messiah, <u>to keep Satan from getting the advantage over us</u>: for we are not ignorant of his wiles and intentions." II Corinthians 2:10* Could the enemy be trying hard to keep God's people offended, judgmental, and critical because he knows the power of forgiveness? Isn't that the message of the cross?

God is calling His people to learn to love and forgive more readily. So let's ask ourselves how we are doing in this area. Is it easy to love others as God does? Not always, but God has given us His Spirit, His grace, to be able to do so. *Matthew 6:14-15* says *"For <u>if you forgive people</u> their trespasses (their reckless and willful sins, leaving them, letting them go, and giving up resentment), your heavenly <u>Father will also forgive you</u>. But <u>if you do not forgive others their trespasses... neither will your Father forgive you your trespasses</u>."* That doesn't mean we lose our salvation, but when we don't forgive, it keeps us from experiencing the abundant life God offers us and blocks the flow of the Spirit to others.

<u>Forgiveness is not a feeling, but it is a decision, a critical one</u>. When we hold onto an offense and refuse to forgive someone, we are <u>locking ourselves into the enemy's domain</u>. Some people suffer illness as well as other problems in life because they need to learn to forgive. When we hold onto unforgiveness in our minds, <u>God's grace is blocked</u>, and we are the ones who suffer. Moreover, we are also keeping the offender from changing, locking them into the prison of their sin. We may think, "But they don't deserve to be forgiven." Neither did we deserve to be forgiven and saved, but God is full of mercy and love, and He extends it readily to any who are ready to receive. <u>When we *choose to forgive*, declaring it over and over until we believe it, we become free and a conduit for God's love and redemptive power</u> to flow to them and reach their heart.

I learned this personally when my brother was murdered by some drug users who were jealous of him. <u>How could I ever forgive their hateful and horrible attacks</u> that took my brother from me and the whole family? In myself, I could not, but as I surrendered my feelings and turned to God, I was able to forgive and to leave these murderers in the hands of the only true Judge, knowing they would one day stand before Him. Did I immediately feel peace? The more I thought of their cruel acts, the more it bothered me. <u>I needed to focus on God's truth and declare my forgiveness many times before I could feel peace in my heart</u>. Forgiveness is not a feeling, but rather an act of the will and a verbal confession that may need to be repeated many times.

2.   Is there anyone you have learned to forgive? If so, explain what you went through.

_____

_____

_____

If not an enemy, is there anyone who has deeply offended you that you are feeling needs to be released from your judgment now?

_____

_____

_____

> **My hope for you during this chapter is that you know with total assurance that the law of God's love controls your life; it leads you to repent and forgive others. It leads you to act and speak more and more as Jesus did. It is the absolute law that governs all that concerns you.**

The connection between obedience and love, trust and friendship...

Our obedience depends on our knowing God's love and that leads us to greater trust and a deeper friendship with Him. In ***John 14:23***, Jesus explains to His disciples*: "if a person really loves Me, he will keep My word—obey my teaching."* This verse used to bother me at times. I knew I wasn't <u>always obedient to everything in God's Word</u>. Did that mean I really didn't love Him? There is clearly a connection between love and obeying the Lord. But does that mean we must strive to obey every facet of what is written in the Word in order to prove our love for God? I don't know about you, but I know I just couldn't do that. <u>That's why we need a Savior</u>. I now see that <u>I prove my love for God by my total dependence on my Savior</u>.

Jesus Himself came to <u>fulfill the law</u> (which mankind could never keep in its entirety). How did he fulfill the law? By laying down His own sinless life so that all who come to Him might be saved. God so loved, that He gave. Christ's surrender and sacrifice led to our having eternal life and to God's law being written on our hearts. In ***Hebrews 8:10*** the Lord says ***"I will <u>imprint My laws upon their</u>***

minds, even upon their innermost thoughts and understanding, and <u>engrave them upon their hearts</u>; and I will be their God and they shall be My people. "God's way is no longer a list of "do's and don'ts" but rather a surrender of our heart to Him.

This reminds me of a big test I faced, a time when I was most deeply led to an act of obedience and trust. I already mentioned this lesson, but allow me to give more detail. While my daughter was in high school, a friend of hers shot himself in the head and died right in front of her. Violence had shattered the peace of our home. Many prayers were uttered for her and others because in her school there was a series of several students' deaths within a month or two. <u>Students began to feel vulnerable and that God was against them</u>. I began to pray for God to use these hard circumstances to save many, to <u>release salvation and revival to her classmates.</u> However, one day a good Christian friend told me about how a relative of hers died and how that caused revival to break out at her school.

I soon began to <u>wonder if maybe God would take my child for the purpose of revival</u>, so I started to pray. I struggled with this thought, like Abraham may have when he was called to sacrifice God's promised son, Isaac. Would God ask that of me? I didn't think so, but <u>I finally reached a place of surrender</u>, recalling God's covenant of love with me. <u>I began to know that I could *trust God*</u> to somehow turn this all into good, no matter what happened to my child, so I went to sleep in peace. The next day while I was preparing for work, I heard the Father's still small voice say to me, "I would never ask that of you." How great is our Father's love for us. In addition, God completed this time of testing by drawing numerous students to a summer Christian youth camp in Malibou, Canada, where there was an outpouring of His saving grace that brought many of my daughter's classmates into His kingdom.

How do we obey the Lord then? Although obedience takes many forms, I believe the heart of <u>obedience must be surrender and trust</u>, laying down one's own thoughts and life, *entrusting* it all into God's hands. Jesus may have been thinking of the price He would soon pay when he said in ***John 15:13-15,*** "***No one has greater love than to <u>lay down (give up) his own life</u> for his friends. <u>You are my friends</u> if you keep on doing the things I command you to do. I do not call you servants any longer, for the servant does not know what his master is doing (working out) ...***" One very important facet of friendship is trust. How can we stay friends with someone we can't trust? Many of life's trials work in us a deeper and <u>deeper trust in the faithfulness of our Lord</u>. Can we trust in the Lord with all our heart and lean not on our own understanding or opinions? ***(Proverbs 3:5-6)*** <u>Does our level of trust demonstrate our level of friendship with Jesus</u>?

Moreover, to be a friend of God, we should also want to spend quality time with Him. We will then <u>begin to think like Him and to understand</u> what He likes and how He would act. We will learn to become more like the old married couple who even finishes each others' sentences because they have learned to think alike.

3. What significance is there to you when Jesus calls you His friend instead of just His servant? *(See John 15:13-15.)*

_____

_____

_____

Now think about your closest friend. What makes your relationship so special? Can you see similarities with that and your relationship with God?

_____

_____

_____

The heart of love to others...

There is a teaching out that we all have different love languages, the way we most often perceive we are loved and demonstrate our love. I've had a question with that, however, because I think we want to see love expressed most in ways that have been lacking. For example, if we never receive gifts from a loved one, maybe that's how we'd like to be loved. Anyway, it's good to remember that <u>there are many different ways to show love to others</u>.

Let's remember that we don't always need to feel love in order to show it. <u>Love (like forgiveness) is a decision or a commitment rather than a feeling</u>. We are called to decide if we are going to treat others well despite how they treat us and whether we can love even if they don't seem to deserve it. That's what unconditional love means. We can choose not to speak negatively (with gossip, for example) but rather to bless others by trying to focus on something positive or good about them. In *Luke 6:27-28* Jesus makes the point even stronger by reminding us to even love our enemies. *"But I say to you who are listening now to Me: (in order to heed, make it a practice to) <u>love your enemies, treat well (do good to, act nobly toward those who detest you and pursue you with hatred. Invoke blessings upon and pray for the happiness</u> of those who curse you, implore God' blessing (favor) upon those who abuse you (who revile, reproach, disparage, and highhandedly misuse you).* It's a pretty big challenge to love others, including the "unlovable" and our enemies, but with God's love in us, it is possible. May God grant us the grace to love our enemies this thoroughly. Such love can only be accomplished through God's powerful grace and mercy.

Jesus said "Love one another as I have loved you." And as He loved (see *I Corinthians 13*), so should we. *II Corinthians 5:14-15* says *"For the <u>love of Christ controls and urges and impels </u>us, because we are of the opinion and conviction that if One died for all, then all died; and He died for all, so that all those who live might <u>live no longer to and for themselves,</u> but to and for Him Who died and was raised again for their sake."* Truly it's the love of God that constrains us to forgive and to love and to live for Him rather than for ourselves.

For any relationship to grow, we need to <u>keep our focus on what is right and good</u>, rather than focusing on what seems "wrong," *Philippians 4:8* is excellent advice: *"For the rest, brethren, whatever is true, <u>whatever is worthy of reverence and is honorable and seemly whatever is lovely and lovable, whatever is kind and winsome and gracious,</u> if there is any virtue and excellence, if there is anything worthy of praise, think on and weigh and take account of these things (<u>fix your minds on them</u>)."* When we humbly keep our focus on judging or evaluating ourselves (and our motives) rather than others, we are free to release God's unconditional love. *I Peter 4:8 advises us, "Above all things have <u>intense and unfailing love for one another, for love covers a multitude of sins</u> (forgives and disregards the offenses of others.)"* When we unconditionally love from our heart, with Christ's love, we are covering the sins of others. Remember it's the demonstration of the Father's love that leads us all to repentance. Do others see this evidence through us?

I remember hearing, "<u>What leaves a heart reaches a heart</u>." So let's keep our focus on our own hearts more than others' word and deeds. We've already briefly discussed how our <u>forgiveness can be a demonstration of God's love</u> toward an enemy or someone who has wronged us. Also previously, we discussed how <u>God can bridge divides if we are willing to surrender</u> our opinions and stop judging others, to focus on good things we have in common rather than our differences. But we are also called to release God's love every day, everywhere we go. <u>Acts of love to strangers and others </u>may simply be a matter of offering a smile or friendly greeting, doing a random act of kindness, or even offering to pray for someone.

4. Is God asking you to surrender a thought or belief to Him in order to release more of His love toward a certain person?

_____

_____

_____

If so, explain who and how you might be able to love that person as Christ does.

_____

_____

_____

Broken promises...

Most of us can remember a significant time when we <u>felt devastated by a broken promise</u>. Maybe it was when you were a child and your parent didn't follow through with something he or she promised you could do or have. Maybe it has happened to you as an adult, in a relationship or on the job. Maybe it has happened to you in the most intimate of relationships, marriage.

"A promise is a promise," used to mean something, but then so did a person's word. "His word makes it as good as done." Do you still feel confidence when someone gives you their word, or do you wonder if this will be just another broken promise? <u>We live in a society of broken commitments and promises</u>. One of the most serious promises, of course, is the marriage commitment, and yet the divorce rate continues to rise, even among Christians. If so many people are not able to keep their marriage covenant, how can we expect that other promises will be kept?

Have you ever wondered why in ***Malachi 2:16*** <u>the Lord says He "hates divorce</u>?" Of course he hates sin, but sometimes innocent parties are involved in divorce, so why does God specifically mention his hatred for divorce? I'm sure <u>God hates divorce largely because He knows the pain</u> it causes everyone, but I think his hatred of this goes beyond that.

<u>God knows *the beauty and power of unity*</u>. The Father, Son, and Holy Spirit are unique persons, yet one. Jesus himself prayed (in ***John 17***) that we may become one with the Father as He was. "United we stand," suggests a powerful truth. <u>Divorce is broken unity</u>, a severing of that which was meant to be one so it goes against the perfect Trinity, the oneness of God.

Moreover, I believe that God specifically hates divorce <u>because it is *the breaking of a covenant agreement*</u>, and that violates the very character of God. <u>God cannot break His promise</u> because He cannot lie (See ***Numbers 23:19***). God's Word is absolute. He is not like man who changes his mind. God is the same yesterday, today, and forever ***(Hebrews 13:8)***, so when He makes <u>a covenant with someone, it can never be broken</u>. Divorce is the breaking of the most serious human covenant of marriage. And we have only to ponder the many references to Christ and His bride to know how much God values the marriage relationship. Divorce is unthinkable to the most holy God and His Son.

It's a wonder that God can show such mercy on a society where broken covenants are so prevalent. We live in a society where many people are discounting absolutes, claiming that everything is relative. Situational ethics has replaced many of our "old-fashioned" beliefs of right and wrong. "If it feels good, it must be okay." "Nothing is absolute or lasting." Instead of holding to an absolute or a covenant, much of <u>our society views situations through the lens of feelings or reasoning</u>. With this type of thinking, it is no wonder that promises or covenants are broken so frequently. <u>Contrast that with God's absolutes that never depend on our feelings or our natural reasoning</u>. What God has said is an unalterable fact.

I know <u>God's perfect will is for unity and healthy relationships</u>. As I previously explained in another chapter, I believe God is able to bridge chasms and heal divisions. However, if both parties are not able to surrender to the cross of Jesus and to crucify their fleshly desires and human "rightness," the chasm may remain. <u>Only God knows</u> how long a spouse is to remain in an unhealthy relationship (that may never be transformed) and only He can decide if or when a spouse is to leave a marriage. I won't presume to give marital advice here, but rather to encourage you to seek God's will and harmony in all your relationships, remembering the power of forgiveness and grace.

5. Explain a broken promise that has affected you considerably.

_____

_____

What do you think was God's perspective on this situation?

_____

_____

_____

Focusing on God's type of love...

Knowing how much God loves us builds our confidence and helps us love others. After all, ***"We love because He first loved us." I John 4:19*** And can we effectively intercede without the love of God in our hearts for the target of our intercession? Jesus says in ***John 15:12-13 "This is My commandment: that you love one another (just) <u>as I have loved you</u>. No greater love (no one has shown stronger affection) than to lay down (give up) his own life for his friends."***

Most likely Jesus is not expecting us to die for someone we love, but rather to give up our own, probably self-focused, way of thinking, speaking, and acting. As usual, God is focusing on the heart of the matter. It's easy to give lip service to love, and perhaps even to be willing to physically die for a loved one, but what about the constant daily opportunities to lay down our lives: to die to our own will or natural understanding... to give up our perspective and surrender to another's point of view...to give another person mercy, grace or forgiveness even when they don't deserve it...or to let go of the notion that we are "right" in a certain matter?

<u>Walking in God's love always means surrender to God, including forgiveness and grace</u>. To check how deeply we are living in God's love, we only need to study ***I Corinthians 13*** and to honestly look deeply into and evaluate our own hearts.

6. Going back to ***I Corinthians 13*** or the last chapter, try to evaluate your love for the following on a scale of 0-10): Your love for God?_____

   For yourself? _____ For family?_____ For friends ?_____

   For the unlovable? _____ For your enemies? _____ For strangers? _____

   How do you think God's love would rate in each of these areas? _____

   What goals might you set for yourself to show more love in any of these areas?

   _____

   _____

   _____

   _____

Abiding in God's Kingdom, subject to His covenant law...

Every country or kingdom is governed by a legal system, sometimes just, sometimes corrupt. God's Kingdom, however, is not only absolutely just and perfect, but it also is governed by one main law, *the law of love.* This law governs God's Kingdom because of the Covenant of Grace He established with us when He gave His only Son, who then gave up His life for us. God's covenant of grace, then, has its foundation in God's love for the world.

In God's Kingdom, all the other principles of government must conform to that one law. Unlike our society of relativisms and variables, God's kingdom is based on absolutes. And all the absolutes in His kingdom are subject to **His supreme law of love.** Since God Himself *is* Love, He cannot rule His kingdom any other way.

I remember when I was learning this truth, I was concerned about my teen-aged daughter. At times it's hard to keep our teen-agers under our loving control. But I saw in my spirit a picture of the boundaries of God's Kingdom around me, and the Holy Spirit spoke to my heart, "Do you see how your daughter is within those boundaries? Then don't worry; My love governs her life as well." That was a turning point in my heart as a mother. My child was more in her Father's loving care than she was in mine. What a relief for my mother's heart. ***Acts 11:14*** gives hope that both you and your household can be saved.

7. Take a minute to picture the people closest to you that you have been praying for. Record a name or two here. _____

    If they know the Lord, can you see them within the boundaries of God's Kingdom, subject to His law of love? If they haven't made that commitment, can you see the cords of God's love extending to them even now, drawing them closer to Him? What does that mean to you?

    _____

    _____

    _____

    _____

Two covenants, two trees, two kingdoms...

Joyce Meyer, in her book *Be Anxious for Nothing*, explains the two covenants or testaments in the Bible: the covenant of works or law and the covenant of grace. "The first covenant is based on man's doing everything on his own, struggling, striving, and laboring to be acceptable to God. That kind of covenant steals joy and peace." (p. 39) In *Galatians chapters 3-4,* Paul is warning believers about returning to that type of bondage. *"Let me ask you this one question: Did you receive the Holy Spirit as the result of obeying the Law and doing its works, or was it by hearing (the message of the Gospel) and believing it? Was it from observing a law of rituals or from a message of faith? " Galatians 3:2*

Joyce continues: "The second covenant, *the covenant of grace*, is based not on what man can do, but on what Christ has already done. Under this covenant, we are justified not by our works or our righteousness, but by our faith and confidence in Christ. That takes the pressure off of us to perform. We can give up our outward efforts and allow God to work through us by the power of His Holy Spirit within us." (p.40) We were, and continue to be, saved by grace through faith as explained in *Ephesians 2:8,* and that grace is God's gift to us daily.

I'm reminded also of the two trees that grew in the Garden of Eden. God clearly forbade Adam and Eve to eat of the tree of the Knowledge of Good and Evil for that would lead them to abide under the Law, bound by human understanding, natural thinking of right and wrong, good and evil. Instead He encouraged them to eat of the Tree of Life, which represents the life we are now free to enjoy in Jesus as we abide under the rule of His love and grace. When we rely too much on our own perspective, our natural understanding, we are partaking of fruit from the wrong tree. That practice will never produce life. *Proverbs 3:5* reminds us *"Trust in the Lord with all your heart, and lean not on your own understanding."*

It also reminds me of the picture I explained in chapter four about <u>our privilege as intercessors to see two kingdoms</u>. We can see someone in the natural realm or the kingdom of darkness, and learn to focus our prayers on them, to bring them to the cross, and then to release them to the power of God's love which draws them into the Kingdom of Light. Remember "Highlight, click and drag?" Perhaps that's a more significant principle than I ever imagined.

<u>So as we intercede, we are to abide under the covenant of grace and love,</u> filled with the Holy Spirit, with our minds renewed by Christ. Then we are positioned correctly and we can feel confident that God is hearing us and will take over from there.

8. How easy is it for you to go from grace into works?

_____

_____

_____

_____

Have you ever noticed how this affects your intercession?

_____

_____

_____

_____

Intercession and God's covenant…

You may still be wondering why God's *covenant of grace and love* is so important to our intercession. <u>My confidence in prayer increases when I reflect on the power of God's unconditional love, demonstrated by Christ's sacrifice that established God's covenant.</u>

<u>Then I know that God always is hearing my prayers</u>, always meeting my needs and the needs of my loved ones, and always being true to His Word. In other words, <u>it is God's covenant of love that sees us through hard times and silent times and that gives us</u> *absolute assurance* <u>as we pray</u>. It is that covenant that <u>enables us to surrender to His perfect will</u> in all situations, for we KNOW, as an absolute fact, that He loves us and will take care of us…no matter what. This is the confidence we have

in Jesus, not because of our own goodness, but because of the power of Christ's blood that sealed the New Covenant.

My personal shield of faith for my loved ones has been ***II Timothy 1:12: "...for I know (perceive, have knowledge of, and am acquainted with) Him Whom I have believed (adhered to and trusted in and relied on), and I am (positively) persuaded that He is able to guard and keep that which has been entrusted to me and which I have committed (to Him) until that day."***

John 15:7 explains what it's like to abide in God's kingdom: "If you live in Me (abide vitally united to Me) and My words remain in you and continue to live in your hearts, ask whatever you will, and it shall be done for you." Our authority and effectiveness as intercessors depends on our covenant relationship with God Himself. As intercessors, married to Christ, we bear His name, and because of His blood covenant with us, we abide under the authority of the Kingdom of God. With His name and by His blood, we have a position in intercession that is *full of the power of God Himself.* Again in ***verse 16*** of that same chapter Jesus said, ***"You have not chosen Me, but I have chosen you and I have appointed you (I have planted you), that you might go and bear fruit and keep on bearing, and that your fruit may be lasting (that it may remain, abide), so that whatever you ask the Father in My Name (as presenting all that I AM), He may give it to you."*** That's the confidence we have as the bride of Christ.

If we ever forget God's covenant of love and the price Jesus paid, our prayers may become dry or empty. We may intercede on behalf of someone for hours and not feel we are touching the Father's heart in the throne room of God. And it may be we are not because *our focus has shifted to the need* (or the person or problem) *rather than to the Answer* to everything.

9.   Have you ever prayed for someone or something and felt your prayers were falling on deaf ears? If so, explain how you felt or responded.

_____

_____

_____

_____

With Christ's death, the whole body of laws was fulfilled. His law of love was established for us when He said on the cross, ***"It is finished." (John 19:30)*** Only in Christ are we able to love as He does. Jesus explained how love was the greatest commandment: ***"You shall love the Lord your God with all your heart and with all your soul and with all your mind (intellect). This is the great (most important, principal) and first commandment. And a second is like it: You shall love your*** *neighbor as (you do) yourself.* <u>*These two commandments sum up and upon them depend all the Law and the Prophets.*</u>*" Matthew 22:37-40*

Peace: the evidence of abiding in the Kingdom of love...

How do we know we are living under God's covenant of love? When our mind and heart is at peace, we know we are enjoying God's law of love. Does God's peace rule in your heart each day? You can always go back to the last chapter to read again about peace, but here are some additional key promises to hold onto.

Jesus is the Prince of Peace (Isaiah 9:6) and Jesus said, "Peace I leave with you; My own peace I now give and bequeath to you. Not as the world gives do I give to you." John 14:27

"Blessed (enjoying enviable happiness, spiritually prosperous—with life-joy and satisfaction in God's favor and salvation, regardless of their outward conditions) are the makers and maintainers of peace, for they shall be called the sons of God!" Mathew 5:9

"Depart from evil and do good; seek, inquire for, and crave peace and pursue (go after) it!" Psalm 34:14

"Great peace have they who love Your law; nothing shall offend them or make them stumble." Psalm 119:165

"You will guard him and keep him in perfect and constant peace whose mind (both its inclination and its character) is stayed on You, because he commits himself to You, leans on You, and hopes confidently in You." Isaiah 26:3

10. What is your favorite promise of peace? When do you most need to know that peace?

_____

_____

_____

_____

The fruit of the Spirit that best <u>demonstrates how securely we abide in God's Kingdom of love is peace</u>. Not only will there be more love for others in our hearts when we abide in God's Kingdom of Love, but our hearts will be at peace. <u>*True peace is what we experience when our souls are in harmony with God's law of love.*</u>

Colossians 3:15 urges us to let the peace of God act as an umpire in our souls. ***"And let the <u>peace (soul harmony which comes) from Christ rule (act as umpire continually)</u> in your hearts (deciding and settling with finality all questions that arise in your minds..."*** That means God's Spirit of <u>peace will decide what's in and what's out</u>, when we are striking out, hitting a foul ball, or scoring a home run. <u>We can tell by the measure of peace that we have whether or not our souls are submitting to the control of God's law of love.</u> Once we experience great peace in our times of intercession, we can <u>shift our prayers from petition to thanksgiving and declaring God's Word with increased authority.</u>

11. Have you come to experience peace as you've been interceding for someone? Describe how that happened for you or write out a prayer here.

_____

_____

_____

_____

And let me conclude with these two powerful blessings:

Numbers 6:24-26 "The Lord bless you and watch guard, and keep you; the Lord make His face to shine upon and enlighten you and be gracious (kind, merciful ,and giving favor) to you; the Lord lift up His (approving countenance upon you and <u>give you peace (tranquility of heart and life continually.</u>"

II Thessalonians 3:16 "Now may the Lord of peace Himself <u>grant you His peace (the peace of His kingdom) at all times and in all ways (under all circumstances and conditions</u>, whatever comes). The Lord (be) with you all."

Chapter 7:
What Grace Is

"Understanding God's Daily Power"

What saving grace means to us...

When I first began to use the Amplified Bible, I noticed right away that grace was defined as "God's unmerited favor." That made a lot of sense to me because I knew I didn't deserve to be saved, but I was because of the grace of God. *Ephesians 2:8 says, "For it is by free grace (God's unmerited favor) that you are saved (delivered from judgment and made partakers of Christ's salvation) through (your) faith. And this (salvation) is not of yourselves (of your own doing, it came not through your own striving), but it is the gift of God; not because of works (not the fulfillment of the Law's demands), lest any man should boast. (It is not the result of what anyone can possibly do, so no one can pride himself in it or take glory to himself.)"* God's saving grace is extended to all of us, but it's not until it's activated by our faith that our souls are saved. So in our discussion of grace, we will also be touching on faith. Even our faith is a gift from God, but we choose to use it or not. If we exercise our faith to receive the free gift of eternal life that God has given to us by grace through His own Son's sacrifice, we are saved, born of His Spirit.

However, salvation is a continuous process. Grace and faith were linked when we were first saved, and they continue to be linked throughout our lives. For that reason, I think we need to carefully consider how both grace and faith affect our daily lives and what they mean in our intercession for others. I think the role of grace, however, has been somewhat misunderstood, undervalued or understated. As Christ followers, we must live under grace rather than law. Moses established the law, but Jesus fulfilled that law by establishing the law of love, grace and truth. (See *John 1:17*.) We can never earn God's grace by obeying the law; it is always a free gift from God because of Jesus' sacrifice.

Let us always remember that grace is not just the favor God once poured out upon us to save us even though we didn't deserve it...it is still operating in our lives daily. We are saved by grace to live by grace. If God's grace saves us from our sins, doesn't it make sense that it would save us or help us with our difficulties? Grace is God's power given freely to us to help us overcome all of life's challenges. *Philippians 2:12* reminds us to work out our own salvation, and to do that we will need to understand the powerful force that God's grace is. I'm encouraged by this simple reminder by Annie Johnson Flint:

"His grace is great enough to meet the great things—

The crashing waves that overwhelm the soul,

The roaring winds that leave us stunned and breathless,

The sudden storms beyond our life's control.

His grace is great enough to meet the small things—

The little pin-prick troubles that annoy,

The insect worries, buzzing and persistent,

The squeaking wheels that grate upon our joy."

1. What is the connection between grace and faith and how are both needed in our prayers?

_____

_____

_____

How might our own efforts keep us from experiencing God's grace?

_____

_____

_____

The promise of grace...

Here is a beautiful promise*: II Corinthians 12:9 "But He said to me, "My grace (My favor and loving-kindness and mercy) is enough to for you (sufficient against any danger and enables you to bear the trouble manfully); for My strength and power are made perfect (fulfilled and completed) and show themselves most effective in (your} weakness."* Does that mean God helps those who help themselves or if we work hard enough, God will help us out? Go back and see the powerful promise in this verse and how it is ours in our weakness more than in our strength or all our human efforts. Could it be that all our striving to have faith actually hinders the flow of God's grace? What we need is just to believe that His grace is sufficient.

When we are weak, we are totally dependent on the strength of another. <u>Our humility is the best attitude to activate grace</u>. ***James 4:6*** is another wonderful promise: ***"But He gives us more and more grace (power of the Holy Spirit, to meet this evil tendency and all others fully). That is why He says, God sets Himself against the proud and haughty, but <u>gives grace (continually) to the lowly (those who are humble enough to receive it.)</u>"*** So the question for us each day is, "Are we humble enough to receive God's grace in every situation?"

I'll never forget what a young student wrote once when asked what grace was. She said, "Grace is like the bubble wrap that protects fragile items."

2.   How do you picture God's grace? Try to describe it or make a comparison here.

_____

_____

_____

Our need for grace...

<u>It's God's grace that changes us, that empowers us to grow as Christians, and that enables us to overcome all difficulties.</u> I'm convinced many of us experience times of great stress, confusion, or even despair because <u>we forget God's provision of grace</u>. When we lean on God's grace to meet every need, we find our strength renewed, our vision restored, and God's peace settled in our hearts and minds. <u>Even as we intercede, we are in need of and empowered by the grace of God</u>. Our prayers and actions may be most effective when they come from a heart of peace and confidence, a heart fully dependent on God's grace.

We need God's grace to enjoy our everyday life. Here are a few other needs we may face:

Grace to overcome loss and disappointment...grace to grieve...grace to work...grace to love the unlovable...grace to forgive the unforgiveable...grace to believe...grace to trust...grace to try new things...grace to not feel alone...grace to reach out to others...grace to obey...the list is endless.

3.   Complete this sentence: Right now, I need more grace to...

_____

_____

_____

The Holy Spirit and God's grace...

Throughout this chapter, we will think deeply about what God's grace is and even what may keep us from experiencing it. Grace is an interesting word. It is defined in many ways from beauty or charm of movement, to courteous good will and mercy, to divine love and protection. <u>Have you ever met anyone who seemed to reflect grace in some way</u>?

I think that my mother was the closest person I've known to embody grace. Her name was Grace and that's how she lived and even how she died. Her gracious acts of kindness, her gentle and loving ways and words, and even her physical poise and beauty reflected a godly nature. Even during the last ten years of her life, while she lost her words with Alzheimer's disease, you could feel the love of God just being in Grace's presence.

I believe Grace may be the most beautiful name ever given to a woman. Sometimes I picture grace as the woman of wisdom described in ***Proverbs 4:8-9*** *"<u>Prize Wisdom</u> highly and exalt her, and she will exalt and promote you; she will bring you to honor when you embrace her. She shall give <u>to your head a</u> <u>wreath of gracefulness; a crown of beauty and glory</u> will she deliver to you."* In fact, there seems to be a connection between wisdom and grace, but I'll let you ponder that on your own.

I have heard that the person of Wisdom in Proverbs refers to Jesus Himself, and similarly I believe God's grace may be referring to the Holy Spirit. The Spirit of God is clearly a person, perhaps not male or female, but there is a connection between the Holy Spirit and grace. <u>Perhaps God's grace is the manifestation of the Holy Spirit ministering to mankind</u>.

Before Jesus ascended into heaven, who did He say would come in his place; who would be sent to be our Helper? He explained in ***John 14:16, "And I will ask the Father, and He will give you another Comforter (Counselor, Helper, Intercessor, Advocate, Strengthener, and Standby), that He may remain with you forever—<u>the Spirit of Truth, Whom the world cannot receive</u> (welcome, take to its heart), because it does not see Him or know and recognize Him, for <u>He lives with you (con-stantly) and will be in you</u>."***

<u>God gives us the grace to live on this earth and to fulfill His purposes</u> through the person of the Holy Spirit. I wonder if we pay enough attention to this wonderful Person of the Trinity. In the 1960's and '70's there was a great outpouring of the Spirit (the Charismatic movement) that brought many of us into the baptism of the Holy Spirit. We received our prayer language and there often were tongues and interpretation in public services. But as the years have passed, I haven't heard as much mentioned about the Holy Spirit, even in "charismatic" circles. The Holy Spirit is still doing a significant work everywhere... in everything... just as God's grace is.

When we face sorrow, He's always near to comfort us. When we face difficulties, He stands near to strengthen and counsel us. He teaches us, directs us, and fills us with the power of God Himself. He helps us with everything, pouring out grace into all situations and revealing God's truth to our minds. And remember in the **John 14** passage, that He is our Intercessor. So when we intercede, we are depending on Him to express our heart to Almighty God. We truly need Him constantly. In essence, <u>I believe God's grace is the power that comes from the Holy Spirit.</u> It is always available to us, just like the Holy Spirit is, but sometimes we forget that truth. We get used to handling our own lives and even to praying as we think best. Do we know He's always standing by to help in any way we need?

I've come to depend on grace to live each day. In times of great trial, when I haven't known how to pray or what to do, I remember **Romans 8:26-27** *"So too <u>the (Holy) Spirit comes to our aid and bears us up in our weakness</u>; for we do not know what prayer to offer, nor how to offer it worthily as we ought, but the Spirit Himself goes to meet our supplication and pleads in our behalf with unspeakable yearnings and groaning too deep for utterance. And He Who <u>searches the hearts of men knows what is in the mind of the (Holy) Spirit</u> (what His intent is) because the Spirit intercedes and pleads (before God) in behalf of the saints according to and in harmony with God's will."* I think, as the challenges of life get very intense, it will be increasingly essential for Christians to receive and use a prayer language from the Holy Spirit.

When I've faced very trying circumstances or just anything that was hard to deal with, I've immediately prayed in the Spirit, but I've also said to God, "More grace, Lord. I need more grace." Or "<u>Great grace, Lord, give me great grace</u>." And it's always been there, sufficient to meet all my needs. Now I'm learning to recognize it every morning and throughout the day. It's like the oil that makes my car's engine function smoothly; it's the oil that helps my spirit and soul function as God intended.

4.   Describe a time when God's grace clearly ministered to you in some way.

_____

_____

_____

_____

_____

My hope in this chapter is simply to emphasize that our prayers, our very lives, depend on the power of the Holy Spirit and the grace of God. I would encourage you to ponder the role of each in your everyday Christian life.

A girl called Grace...

I'd like to explain a bit more about what grace is and is not. I hope to do that by sharing a special time in my life and story with you. The summer of 2009 was when I learned to abide daily in God's grace. I was faced with the <u>daunting (if not impossible) challenge of cleaning out the family home</u> (Grace's home or the house of Grace, she'd lived in for sixty years) in order to put it on the market and move out of town. There was no choice in this matter because of a huge economic crisis my family faced, yet as I lived there then, I was quite alone in how to go about this task that was my responsibility. It was truly overwhelming, sixty years of my family's stuff...sixty years of dear memories. The whole process was one I never thought I could handle. And but for God's grace...I never could have.

As I prayed, I learned to commit the whole project to God, and every day I'd just do as much as I could, <u>one step at a time. The impossible task actually progressed quite easily</u>. I packed, painted, sorted, donated, and dumped....then I packed, painted, sorted, donated, and dumped all over again...and again. When I needed physical help, it was there. Even my gardener agreed to clean out the nastiest places of the old garage. Every day I came to know that I couldn't possibly tackle the work at hand without the grace of God. I learned to ask for "great grace" when the burden seemed overwhelming. And great grace was always there.

There's an old hymn by Annie J. Flint that is so true: *"<u>He giveth more grace when the burdens grow greater</u>, He sendeth more strength when the labors increase; to added afflictions He addeth His mercy, to multiplied trials, His multiplied peace."* The hymn ends with *"His love has no limits, <u>His grace has no measure</u>, His power no boundary known unto men; For out of His infinite riches in Jesus He giveth, and giveth, and giveth again."* That hymn speaks a profound truth about <u>who God is and how He is there for us at all times</u>.

5. What is the burden that weighs most heavily on your heart today?

_____

_____

_____

_____

_____

In the midst of the moving challenge I faced, God actually gave me times of rest. He put a story in my heart and gave me the quiet time to write it. I share it with you now because it expresses my heart about God's grace perhaps better than any other words I could write. There is sometimes <u>misunderstanding about grace by those who abuse it and use it to entitle</u> them to do whatever they want. There are also many <u>others who keep trying to work at life instead</u> of learning the secret of depending on and abiding in God's free grace. This story describes these different approaches.

My story is called, "The Girl Called Grace," and I wrote it on July 14, 2009, as I cleaned out the House of Grace. I wrote it in honor of my mother, Grace, who taught me so much about living in grace and extending it to others. This is the story:

The Girl Called Grace

Three little girls lived on the same street but hardly knew each other. They saw each other from a distance, but none dared to approach the other. They went to the same school but were in different classes.

One day the little blonde girl, named Bon-Bon, began to feel very lonely. She had finished all her chores, which were many, and found herself longing to have a friend and knowing that making a friend had not been an easy task for her. "I can't see my good friend, Captive, anymore because she's being punished for not doing all her parents expected of her...now who will be my friend?" Bon-Bon lamented.

The days passed and blonde Bondage (which was in fact her official name) grew increasingly lonely and tired of working. "Maybe if I work extra hard, it will make me feel fulfilled and so proud that I won't long for a friend any more." So, little Bon-Bon began to work super hard around her house. She cleaned and re-cleaned, trying to make old things look new and spotless. But the more she worked, the more frustrated she became. "The harder I work, the more I see that needs to be done...the more effort I put out, the more seems to be needed... and I'm getting so tired. Even if I work my fingers to the bone, it is never enough." So with these troubling thoughts, Bon-Bon kept at it, night and day, despite her anguish, her exhaustion, and her increasing sense of hopelessness.

Just down the street in a rather unkempt little house lived Freebie, a red-haired little girl who seemed to have no cares in the world. She was part of a family of free-spirits, who hardly ever worked, but just catered to their desires for fun and entertainment. "This is the life." Freebie's mom would often tell her, and for a while the girl agreed that it was great fun to stay up late, to play all day and all night, and to feast on ice cream and french fries. But lately, Freebie had begun to feel uneasy and bored with her life style. Her stomach had begun bothering her and she found she was beginning to feel tired all the time. Besides this, it was bothering her even more that she could not find a friend who also enjoyed such freedoms.

"What good is it to have all this pleasure if I have no one to share it with? And, to be honest, I'm getting a little tired of having no rules; knowing I can do anything, makes everything pretty boring...Sometimes I wonder if anyone really cares about me. No one seems to love me enough to show me how to keep from getting sick to my stomach or how to become truly satisfied. Maybe nothing in life really satisfies...How I wish someone could help me." So Freebie continued to go on as she had been shown, doing as she pleased and never thinking of how it was bringing her down further and further, like the spinning vortex of a whirlpool.

Across the street in a cozy little white house lived the third girl name Grace. Her soft brown hair flowed down her back and added to the gentleness her face expressed. She too was wanting the companionship of a new friend, but unlike the others, she didn't feel in a desperate need of company. Instead she felt the desire to share with others and to help others in any way she could.

When she woke up every morning, she would spend time with her best friend. That always seemed to lighten any load she was carrying...whether it was a load of ordinary concerns or heavy weights like sorrow, fear, or doubt. She never went away from their time together without feeling refreshed and ready to face the day. So, with a song in her heart, Grace went about her daily chores.

"I've noticed two girls who live on this street, and I'm wondering if it's time to get to know them. They both look lonely and empty inside although they always seem busy. How curious to be busy, busy, busy, but empty at the same time. I'd like to understand how this could be," pondered Grace one morning when she met with her friend.

So that afternoon she decided to invite both Bon-Bon and Freebie over for a tea party. "I've been wanting to get to know you both and what fun it'll be to have a real tea party in my back yard!" exclaimed Grace to the other girls. Freebie was excited to be invited to share a new experience and maybe get a new friend, but Bon-Bon wasn't so sure.

"I have so very much to do, I don't see how I could come." But after some per- suading on the parts of both Grace and Freebie, Bon-Bon put down her dust mop and joined the other two.

The three little girls sat on small chairs around a pretty table all set with dainty cups and delicate flowers. "Wow, this is really nice," exclaimed both guests almost simultaneously. Grace began to serve scrumptious open-faced sandwiches and soft, melt-in-your mouth cookies. "This is delicious," offered Bon-Bon, "it must have taken you hours to get all this ready."

"Oh, not really," replied Grace. Once I got the idea, it was super easy to put it all together. And I had such fun thinking of how it might bless you two."

"It sure does," added Freebie. "It's such good food, it makes my stomach feel so much better, and I can almost feel new energy coming into my body."

"That's the way it should be," explained Grace. "Life is meant to be enjoyed, but we must remember what's helpful for our bodies because we do, after all, have to live in them for quite a while."

"You mean we can overdo things, even good things?" both girls questioned."

"Of course," replied Grace. "Life is meant to be enjoyed. It's not always rules and work (that just wears us out), and it's not just doing what feels good at the moment because that can really harm us and make us unable to truly enjoy anything."

"So it's a matter of balance, right?" asked Bon-Bon who was very seriously listening to this discussion.

"Not exactly," explained their wise little hostess. "I've found that although balance is good, even necessary, it's not enough. I've discovered a secret that makes everything better. Hard things become easier and heavy things become lighter."

"You have to be kidding," blurted Freebie. "I've been doing everything the easy way and neglecting every heavy burden, but I'm just getting more and more worn out. How could there be a secret to enjoying life more and living more freely?"

"Yes, Grace, please tell us your secret because I feel I can't go on much longer working as hard as I do. I'm just exhausted and not enjoying life at all."

"Okay, my friends. The secret is only yours if you spend time with my special friend. I can introduce you to Him if you'd like. Once you know Him, you'll see that He pours something out upon you that instantly lightens your load, lifts your cares, and brings joy to your heart."

"Really?" both girls exclaimed in curious disbelief.

"Yes, it's true. At first I didn't realize this oil was mine to receive and use each day. I thought it was only for special occasions, but lately He's been showing me that I can receive this everyday for every need I face... whether it's a horrible crisis or just an ordinary task at hand. And every time I let His oil cover me, all the negative parts of life slide right over me. And besides that, I get incredible energy to complete all that I have to do each day. To top it off, this wonderful substance puts a new song in my heart and causes me to feel peace and joy no matter what I'm doing."

"Oh, if I could only experience such restful ease," cried Bon-Bon.

"Yes, and it sounds so much better than just doing my own thing, which has been draining me of all joy in living."

"Well, my friends, the best part of all is that my Friend wants me to extend this fragrant oil to everyone I'm with. So today I give you His oil of joy called grace so that you might come to know my Friend and how to live an abundant and exciting life every day. All you have to do is receive this grace. It's completely free for the asking...but you must take it."

So the two little girls both lifted their faces and said with one voice, "Yes, please fill us with His grace so that we too may live life more fully."

And that's how both Bon-Bon and Freebie became close friends of Grace. Over the years, they grew to love her more and more, to learn from her, and to depend on her when life got tough...and even when life was normal. Yes, Grace became their treasured friend forever, and she never let them down.

6. Which of the 3 girls do you identify with the most?_____ and why?

_____

_____

_____

_____

What was the key to Grace's abundant life of peace, joy, and other-centeredness?

_____

_____

_____

Here is a description of how the Spirit of the Lord, the Spirit of Grace, empowered Jesus. ***"To grant (consolation and joy* to those who mourn in Zion—to give them an ornament (a garland or diadem) of *beauty instead of ashes, the oil of joy instead of mourning,* the *garment (expressive) of praise instead of a heavy burdened, and failing spirit*—that they may be called oaks of righteousness (lofty, strong, and magnified, distinguished for uprightness, justice, and right standing with God), the planting of the Lord, that He may be glorified." Isaiah 61:3*** So let us also move in that Spirit, enjoying the marvelous gift of grace, as we minister to others.

What a Friend...

God is truly able to give us beauty for ashes, strength for weakness, and joy for everyday living, but do we always remember to cast al our cares upon Him? *I Peter 5:7 "Casting the whole of your care (all your anxieties, all your worries, all your concerns, once and for all) on Him, for He cares for you affectionately and cares about you watchfully."* And I would add "because you are His personal concern." Why do we wait until we are at "the end of our rope" before we do this?

Remember the old hymn: *What a Friend We Have in Jesus?* Here are some phrases: *"all our sins and griefs to bear...what a privilege to carry everything to God in prayer? O what peace we often forfeit, O what needless pain we bear, all because we do not carry everything to God in prayer."* All three verses of this are vital to our spiritual health.

I like Joyce Meyer's advice that sometimes we just need to step aside and have a little meeting with ourselves. That's what we should do from time to time every day. Come away from life's cares, realize what we are thinking, and then call out to our best Friend for help. Perhaps the best prayer is the simplest: "Help me, Lord. I need you so much."

7. What would you like to share with your Friend right now? What situation do you need help with most? He's listening.

_____

_____

_____

Every day we make hundreds of choices, most of which are subconscious. We choose to fret or stew on a problem or situation, we try to ignore it hoping it will go away, or we choose to give it to God and trust Him to give us the grace to endure or to set us free from it altogether. It seems obvious what the best option is.

Joshua 24:15 reveals we can be either siding with the enemy of our souls or depending on the grace of God in every circumstance. *"And if it seems evil to you to serve the Lord, choose for yourselves this day whom you will serve, whether the gods which your fathers served on the other side of the River, or the gods of the Amorities, in whose land you dwell; but as for me and my house, we will serve the Lord."* Perhaps when we don't "take it to the Lord in prayer" we are making a dangerous choice. It is time to choose once and for all who we will serve, in every aspect of every day. I choose God and his abundantly loving grace.

8. Why not write a declaration here that you are choosing to serve the Lord and follow Him? Does this declaration include your whole household?

_____

_____

_____

_____

_____

_____

Evidence of God's grace...

Have you ever called out to God for help when doing an ordinary task and actually been surprised at how easy the task then became? This happened to me recently when I was having trouble hanging a large mirror. Now I'm beginning to catch on that God cares about the little things in life, the daily challenges or chores, as well as the big crisis moments in our lives.

How do we know we are experiencing God's grace? Life becomes easier. The good times become better and the bad moments become lighter. I've already talked a lot about peace, but to me <u>my soul peace is the biggest indicator that I am abiding in God's provision of grace</u>.

Perhaps you remember seeing the picture of peace. It was of a small bird, sheltered in the protection of the cleft of a rock while all around it raged a violent storm. That's what peace is. That's the promise of **Psalm 91:1 *"He who <u>dwells in the secret place</u> of the Most High shall <u>remain stable and fixed</u> under the shadow of the Almighty (Whose power no one can withstand)."***

9. What situation or concern is keeping you from experiencing deep soul peace? Take it to the Lord in prayer.

_____

_____

_____

<u>God's grace gives us favor with people, and favor means approval, support, and liking</u>. As we grow into a greater likeness to Jesus, we acquire more of his favor. ***"And Jesus increased in wisdom (in***

broad and full understanding) and in stature and years, and in favor with God and man. Luke 2:52 <u>Knowing God's grace and favor in our lives, brings God glory</u>. *"So that we might be to the praise and the commendation of <u>His glorious grace (favor and smercy)</u>, which He so freely bestowed on us in the Beloved. In Him we have redemption (deliverance and salvation) through His blood, the remission (forgiveness) of our offenses (shortcomings and trespasses), in accordance with the riches and <u>the generosity of His gracious favor</u>, which He lavished upon us in every kind of wisdom and understanding (practical insight and prudence)." Ephesians 2:6-8*

Other <u>evidence of God's grace is the manifestation of any of the fruit of the Spirit</u> listed in *Galatians 5:22.* What fruit do have most need of with current circumstances? *Love, joy, peace, patience, kindness, goodness, faithfulness, gentleness, or self-control?* Of course, we need and want to experience all of these, but there may be one that stands out to you right now. Or perhaps you need other qualities like hope or faith. In subsequent chapters I will talk more about these essentials.

10. What fruit of the Spirit to you want to experience in the situation you mentioned in question 9?

_____

_____

_____

Bending but not broken...

While I was writing this section, I listened to Joel Osteen teach on the power of bouncing back. We all go through tough times, but <u>God gives resiliency to Christians</u>, the ability to bounce back from any difficulty. He used <u>the illustration of a palm tree</u> that faces hurricane winds but doesn't break. Instead it bends and bows down when in the midst of a storm. Other trees are up-rooted, even the strongest may fall during a hurricane. But not only does the palm tree survive, its roots actually become stronger.

Isn't that a beautiful picture of God's grace? How it sways so gracefully in the breeze and bends so lowly in the storms. May we each choose to become like the palm tree. As soon as I finished the program and opened my Bible, I "happened" upon this verse:

Psalm 92:12-15 "The (uncompromisingly) <u>righteous shall flourish like the palm tree</u> (be long-lived, upright, useful, and fruitful)...planted in the house of the Lord, they shall flourish in the courts of our God. (<u>Growing in grace) they shall still bring forth fruit in old age;</u> they shall be full of sap (of spiritual vitality) and (rich in the) verdure (of trust, love, and contentment). (<u>They are living memorials) to show that the Lord is upright and faithful to His promises;</u> He is my Rock, and there is no unrighteousness in Him."

May we each choose to live as a righteous palm tree, growing in grace every day to the glory of our Father. Here's a simple prayer for each day:

Lord, give me the daily grace
To abide in that sweet place
Of knowing Your ways are best
And keeping my heart at rest.

11. Write a prayerful declaration here, that you are choosing to look for and live in God's grace each day.

_____

_____

_____

_____

_____

_____

II Corinthians 12:9 explains that God's grace is always sufficient for all our needs, and that it is made perfect in our weakness. The verse concludes with Paul's conclusion: *"Therefore, I will all the more __gladly glory in my weaknesses__ and infirmities, that __the strength and power of Christ (the Messiah) may rest (yes, may pitch a tent over and dwell) upon me__."*

Chapter 8:
What Grace Does

"Dealing with Life's Challenges"

Extending God's grace to others...

God not only wants us to abide in His grace and to intercede in His grace, but also to impart His grace to others through our thoughts, words, and actions. Extending grace means letting offenses go: forgiving and forgetting. I previously wrote about the power of forgiveness and why it may be one of the most important things we as Christians need to do. But here, I'd like to focus on the little things that don't seem to warrant our forgiveness. Think with me a bit about small offenses or injustices that you might forget about without actually forgiving.

We, human beings, have the natural ability to put things out of our mind that we don't like. Some of us have "swept things under a rug" in our minds so often that our subconscious minds are crowded with these things. Here, I'm talking about things we may say (or pretend) don't bother us like an unkind word or thoughtless action of another. We like to imagine that these things don't bother us, but they may actually be accumulating inside us, building up much like a pressure cooker does. We cannot live healthy lives with this going on.

We need to continually ask God to search our hearts and reveal what is in them. God isn't just interested in what we say and do, but why. He looks in our hearts to see our motives, which may be quite hidden. ***Psalm 139:23-24*** says, ***"Search me (thoroughly), O God, and know my heart! Try me and know my thoughts! And see if there is any wicked or hurtful way in me, and lead me in the way everlasting."***

When we don't open our hearts regularly to God, we may hold onto subconscious thoughts that cause us to speak or act in ungodly ways. For intercession, and really all ministry, to be effective we need to let grace flow out of pure hearts. Often I am drawn to David's heartfelt ***Psalm 51,*** which he prayed after he sinned. I won't quote the whole chapter here but mention that he cried out for God's mercy, to know truth in his inner being, and wisdom in his inmost heart ***(verse 6).*** He sought God to cleanse his heart and renew the joy of his salvation. I think this psalm reveals one reason why David was a man after God's own heart. (See ***I Samuel 13:14***.)

How can we experience all the blessings of God's grace, and extend it to others, if we actually have <u>ungracious thoughts hidden in our hearts</u>? So if we have trouble being gracious to anyone in word or deed, it's a signal to ask God to purify our hearts and then fill our minds with God's truth. ***Psalm 119:11*** advises us ***"your word have I laid up in my heart, that I might not sin against You."*** Even though I'm not devoting an entire chapter in this study to the power of God's Word, <u>I've tried to include much of God's truth throughout these pages</u>, and I hope you will read and reread these wonderful words. <u>When God fills our hearts and minds with His truth, we become clean vessels</u> to impart God's grace to others. God gives us opportunities constantly to extend His grace to the people we encounter and relate to each day, so let us be ready with open and pure hearts.

1. How could you extend God's grace in the following situations?

    Your husband forgot your anniversary (even with your subtle hints), you could…

    _____

    _____

    Your co-worker blamed you for a huge problem that occurred at work, but you knew it was someone else's fault, you could…

    _____

    _____

    Your teen-age daughter doesn't relate to you as you'd like, you could…

    _____

    _____

    Your aging father called but forgot to thank you for all the work you did for him, you could…

    _____

    _____

    A person just cut in front of you in the long line at the grocery store, you could…

    _____

    _____

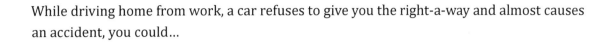

While driving home from work, a car refuses to give you the right-a-way and almost causes an accident, you could…

_____

_____

Maybe minor offenses, but still offenses. The list could go on and on. We've all been offended in many ways by the words or actions of others. Now, let's be honest about our heart's response. We probably don't always bless these "transgressors," but <u>inwardly judge or condemn them.</u> Instead of extending grace to them, we feel reluctant to forgive and forget…because they just don't deserve it. But what is grace? God's undeserved favor. Ouch. We really don't have a choice.

Remember God looks at the heart. If we harbor unforgiveness toward anyone, it acts like a poison in our hearts. Extending grace to those who offend us in any way, is putting the "power of the Gospel" into practice. Maybe we do this by responding as Christ would or just by <u>surrendering our natural reactions to the Lord and allowing Him to give us peace in our hearts</u>.

It's not just about pleasing ourselves or others in this life, but rather <u>it's all about pleasing God</u>. *"Whatever may be your task, work at it heartily (from your soul), as (something done) <u>for the Lord and not for men</u>, knowing (with all certainty) that it is from the Lord (and not from men) that you will receive the inheritance which is your (real) reward." Colossians 3:23-24*

> **My hope in this chapter is to show you how God's grace actively works to improve your relationships and to help you overcome life's difficulties.**

The power of the tongue…

There is a clear connection between extending grace and blessing other people. We bless others by <u>repenting of the negative thoughts we have in our heart toward them and by expressing the opposite or more positive thoughts</u>. We are bound to have countless opportunities each day to <u>choose blessing or cursing</u>. Using the "curse" word may seem extreme, but if we are not blessing others, aren't we leaving them in a fallen world, subject to our enemy's strategies and lies? We are all responsible for the thoughts in our hearts and the words we speak.

The book of *James* gives us clear teaching on the power of our words to bless or to curse. *James 3:10-11 "<u>Out of the same mouth come forth blessing and cursing</u>. These things, my brethren, <u>ought not to be so</u>. Does a fountain send forth (simultaneously) from the same opening fresh water and bitter?"* Before that in *verse 8*, James says *"But the human tongue can be tamed by no man. It is a restless (undisciplined, irreconcilable) evil, <u>full of deadly poison</u>."* Jesus said *"But I tell you, on the day of judgment men will have to <u>give account for every idle (inoperative,</u>*

nonworking) word they speak." And may we never forget that ***by our words we shall be condemned and by our words we shall be justified*** (*See Matthew 12:36-37*). I believe all that we say (and even think) serves either to <u>build up (edify) or to tear down (destroy)</u>.

So what is God's view on the rampant use of social media, where we are given blatant "freedom of speech" to utter any blessing or any curse that we feel at the moment? I won't even explore that subject here, but let me just say that <u>repentance is needed throughout our world today for the lies and curses that are posted.</u> God surely does not consider these things to be idle or without consequences. <u>May God help us guard our ears and our eyes, and surrender our inmost thoughts and words in order to edify and bless others.</u>

2. Take a moment here to record a blessing, or word of encouragement, to someone.

_____

_____

Nullifying the grace of God…

Even though God makes His grace freely available and pours it our abundantly, it is possible for us to block that flow. It's not always blocked by overt sin; <u>often it's our striving or an inner sin like our judgments or unbelief that frustrates or nullifies God's grace.</u> Frustration is what we feel when a goal is blocked, and all our human efforts and striving to measure up to God's perfection only cause us frustration. We cannot do what only God's grace was meant to do. I imagine <u>God may also feel frustrated</u> when we do that and when He cannot move as He would like because of our heart issues or our works of the flesh that hinder the flow of His grace. <u>Nullifying God's grace is perhaps worse</u>; it's like canceling out the power and effectiveness of God's grace. Why would we ever want to do that? But if we're honest, we may actually do that at times.

The following verse (***Galatians 2:21***) explains what a grief it must be to God when we frustrate His grace: ***(Therefore, I do not treat God's gracious gift as something of minor importance and defeat its very purpose); I do not set aside and invalidate and frustrate and nullify the grace (unmerited favor) of God. For if justification (righteousness, acquittal from quilt) comes through (observing the ritual of) the Law, then Christ (the Messiah) died groundlessly and to no purpose and in vain. (His death was then wholly superfluous.)***

Let me clarify a bit more. One great obstacle to the flow of grace must be our negative thoughts or words as explained previously. <u>A similar hindrance, however, is our *unbelief*.</u> ***Matthew 13:38 explains "And He did not do many works of power there, because of their unbelief (their lack of faith in the divine mission of Jesus).***

To avoid the enemy's lies or the deceptive thinking of the world, we might pray daily, "Help, Lord, my unbelief," presenting ourselves before His throne of grace and <u>allowing our minds to become vessels of His grace</u>. ***"Do not be conformed to this world** (this age), (fashioned after and adapting to its external, superficial customs), but be transformed (changed) by the (entire) <u>renewal of your mind</u> (by its new ideals and its new attitude), so that you may prove (for yourselves) what is the good and acceptable and perfect will of God, even the thing which is good and acceptable and perfect (in His sight for you).* (* See **Romans 12:1-2**.)* Our minds can be God's richest ground for faith or a battlefield for our enemy.

<u>Another obstacle that nullifies God's grace must be our "works."</u> Sometimes when we are so busy "doing" we forget our "being" in the presence of the Lord. We keep running our "engine" until the oil dries up or clogs our system. We may ignore the "oil light" and let our heart's engine break down. And we can't wait 3,000 miles to get a grace-oil change! Remember the parable of the ten virgins **(Matthew 25)** and how only half of them had enough oil in their lamps when the bridegroom came for them? May God help us stay filled with the oil of God's grace every day until He returns.

Romans 7:6 reminds us that ***"we are discharged from the Law and have terminated all intercourse with it, having died to what once restrained and held us captive.*** "<u>We are to live under the covenant of grace rather than law.</u> In **Galatians**, Paul exhorts believers not to return to the bondage of the law. He even spoke of how he had been "crucified with Christ" even while he lived. ***"I have been crucified with Christ (in Him I have shared His crucifixion); <u>it is no longer I who live, but Christ (the Messiah) lives in me</u>; and the life I now live in the body I live by faith in (by adherence to and reliance on and complete trust in) the Son of God, who loved me and gave Himself up for me." Galatians 2:20.***

This verse precedes the one mentioned earlier about Paul's not treating God's gracious gift as something of minor importance that can be set aside or invalidated. This explanation from the Amplified Bible makes it quite clear that <u>God expects us to abide in His grace</u> and not deny it. Once again, this depends on our surrender, our willingness to die to our self and to live in Christ's power.

"But by the grace (the unmerited favor and blessing) of God <u>I am what I am, and His grace toward me was not (found to be) for nothing (fruitless and without effect)</u>. In fact, I worked harder than all of them (the apostles) <u>though it was not really I, but the grace</u> (the unmerited favor and blessing) of God which was with me. I Corinthians 15:10

3. Can you think of a time when you may have felt the grace of God was being frustrated? If so, please explain how you were able to get back into God's grace.

_____

_____

Releasing God's grace into our prayers...

If indeed we are saved by grace (through our faith), it makes sense that grace is the key to all life and to all persons or situations where salvation is needed. In my mind, I am seeing grace also as the *power of the Gospel.* We've heard that phrase, but have you pondered what that means to your daily life and prayers? Think about the Good News (Gospel) of Jesus Christ and how that reality may transform how you pray and intercede.

Let me explain more what I mean here. Perhaps we are interceding for a person who needs to be saved from self or sin. We can share God's truth with that person, and we can repeatedly ask God to save him, but there may be no change. There are a number of reasons for this, and we might ask why. Perhaps it's just a matter of timing. God is never late, but often His times and ways are quite different from ours. Or perhaps the missing ingredient in our intercession is God's grace. As I wrote earlier, it's not that God is withholding His grace, but rather that we may be blocking the flow of it by our own thought patterns or unbelief, our persistent or ignorant efforts, or our lack of total sur-render to the Lord. If we know we are vessels of God's grace and if we are not nullifying that grace by our own thoughts or efforts, we should be able to release God's grace into our prayers for others. Our faith plus God's grace may bring salvation and breakthrough.

What does it feel like to us when we release God's grace into our prayers or situations? Releasing grace may change how we see or feel and how we pray. We may begin to feel the peace and hope of God with greater confidence of faith, knowing our words align with those of our Lord. When we know our prayers are led by the Holy Spirit, we impart words of grace in intercession to that person or into that situation. Our words will be positive, loving, and compassionate, although perhaps firm. Our prayers, seasoned with grace, may also be filled more with praise and thanksgiving. They demon-strate the depth of our trust in God.

Perhaps it's easier to recognize when our words and prayers are not seasoned with God's grace. Since our words come from our hearts, we need to impart grace instead of fear, worry, guilt, condemnation, judgment, self-interest, self-pity, doubt, or unbelief. We never want to be interceding for others with these ugly feelings contaminating our heart. When we recognize these attitudes, we'd be better off first focusing on ourselves, rather than the other person or the situation we're praying for. When our hearts are pure, our prayers and words are seasoned with grace and that's when God's saving power is released through us.

4. Explain how grace can activate our prayers. What then is the power of the Gospel and how does it transform our Christian lives and prayers?

_____

_____

_____

_____

_____

_____

Grace on the battlefield...

Every intercessor will no doubt be faced with enemy opposition. God's grace gives us the power to overcome the attacks of the enemy of our souls. That is what we should remember when we pray and even when we are around people who might offend us. We should always remember that people aren't the problem or the enemy. Satan is. And how we face these attacks should also be in the spirit, rather than in our flesh. ***"For though we walk (live) in the flesh, we are not carrying on our warfare <u>according to the flesh</u> and using mere human weapons, <u>For the weapons of our warfare are not physical (weapons of flesh and blood), but they are mighty before God for the overthrow and destruction of strongholds.</u>" (II Corinthians 10:3-4)***

<u>A stronghold is a place in our hearts where we have allowed Satan to take control</u>. It may be formed over many years as we hold onto negative thoughts and unforgiveness, probably because of abusive or unjust happenings. It is <u>often a hidden place of deception and lies</u> where we have not allowed the light of God's truth to penetrate. But God's Word and His grace can reveal the enemy's strategies and set us free from this bondage.

Many have written on how Satan's battlefield is our mind, and I would encourage you to study such truth until you know there are no enemy strongholds within your heart. As we intercede for others, <u>let us be aware that they may have powerful strongholds in their hearts that God's truth can overthrow</u>. We may see this and share Bible verses, but most of our effort should be in prayer. When a person's mind has been greatly deceived, it may be wiser to declare truth in our intercessory prayers and depend on the Holy Spirit to lead us in our intercession. For it is the Spirit of God Who always sets people free, and ***"Greater is He that is in us than he that is in the world." I John 4:4***

The first Christian book I read many years ago was *Prison to Praise* by Merlin Carothers. That book presented the concept of thanking God and praising Him in the midst of difficult situations, not because we appreciated the situation but because we appreciated Who God was to us. God actually inhabits our praises (See *Psalm 22:3*.) That truth powerfully delivers us from the prison of hopelessness.

When I was first baptized in the Holy Spirit, there was quite an emphasis on spiritual warfare. We often would spend much of our prayer time "binding and loosing" and putting Satan in his place. (See *Matthew 18:18*.) Although I'm sure God calls us to do this at times, I think too much emphasis on this may lead us more into "works" instead of abiding in His grace.

Before I go on, let me emphasize that in Old Testament times of battle, the <u>worshippers were sent ahead of the troops.</u> (See *II Chronicles 20:1-24*.) The power of praise and worship in our warfare praying cannot be overstated. When we let go of our natural thinking and enter God's courts with praise and thanksgiving, even allowing ourselves to get caught up in worshipping our wonderful Lord, we are in the best position for warfare. *Psalm 100:4* urges us: ***"<u>Enter into His gates with thanksgiving and a thank offering and into His courts with praise</u>! Be thankful and say so to Him, bless and affectionately praise His name!"***

<u>When the battle rages around you, it's the best time to worship.</u> Chuck Pierce has written a powerful book called *Worship Warrior*, and I'd highly recommend it. I also recommend that you play worship music 24/7 when needed to fill your home and heart with truth. Satan cannot stand to be in that atmosphere.

5. What do you think spiritual warfare means and why do we often face it.

_____

_____

6. What have you found to be most effective in your spiritual warfare prayers?

_____

_____

_____

Grace in the Courtroom of heaven...

Not long ago a teaching by Robert Henderson emerged in the body of Christ about *The Courtroom of Heaven.* As soon as I heard that title, I knew God was leading us into an important truth, which I encourage you to investigate on your own. The premise of this teaching is that we <u>should enter the</u> <u>courtroom to get God's verdict before we spend all our energy on the battlefield</u>, waging all manner of spiritual warfare. I will not presume to do this subject justice here, but I must mention it because it offers a very essential aspect to our intercession. <u>It's a teaching that relies on God's grace and mercy</u> <u>to release justice.</u> Leaning on God's grace, instead of waging war on the battlefield, makes spiritual warfare easier. After all, it's never our words or power, but God's that brings solutions. ***Zechariah 4:5b "<u>Not by might, nor by power, but by My Spirit</u> (of Whom the oil is a symbol) says the Lord of hosts."***

As intercessors, <u>we are allowed to enter the courtroom of Almighty God</u>, the only wise Judge. <u>Jesus</u> <u>comes with us as our legal defense</u>, our Advocate, who is able to save to the uttermost ***(Hebrews 7:25)*** and, of course, <u>Satan is present as our accuser.</u> ***Revelation 12:10*** speaks of Satan's final end ***"for the accuser of our brethren, he who keeps bringing before our God charges against them day and night, has been cast out!"*** But until that day, <u>we may often be contending with our enemy</u> <u>in God's courtroom.</u>

As I said before, we should think honestly a minute about what is in our hearts. Are we actually <u>over-</u> <u>come by the enemy's lies, or do we instead believe the truth of God's saving grace for ourselves and</u> <u>for those we pray for?</u> Our words and attitudes reveal what is really in our heart.

So how do we pray in the courtroom of heaven? What are the weapons of our warfare that will defeat the enemy of our souls and the enemy of those we may be lifting u in prayer? ***Revelation 12:12*** reveals how we have victory in our Christian lives. ***"And they have overcome (conquered) him by means of the <u>blood of the Lamb and by the utterance of their testimony</u>, for they did not love and cling to life even when faced with death (holding their lives cheap till they had to die for their witnessing)."*** We overcome by the <u>blood of the Lamb and the words of our mouth</u> that come from a pure heart and agrees with God's perfect will.

With that in mind, let us consider further the courtroom of heaven. As we intercede, we enter God's courtroom knowing that <u>our righteousness (or the righteousness of a loved one) is but filthy rages</u> ***(Isaiah 64:6)*** and that even though we (or they) may be saved, none of us are yet made perfect. So what hope is there that the Judge will not issue a <u>guilty verdict</u> for us? We are in ourselves truly guilty.

If the accuser's lies hold some truth, how can we ever be declared not guilty in God's courtroom? As we pray, we should again ask God to search our hearts. <u>Does the accuser have any legal right to</u> <u>attack or has repentance taken place?</u> Satan has no legal right to anything that has been put under the blood of Jesus. ***"If we (freely) admit that we have sinned and confess our sins, <u>He is faithful</u> <u>and just (true to His own nature and promises) and will forgive our sins (dismiss our lawless-</u> <u>ness)</u> and (continually) cleanse us from all unrighteousness (everything not in conformity to His will in purpose, thought, and action."*** *I John 1:9* We can even repent on behalf of someone else until they are able to do so. <u>We do this by acknowledging our sin (or their sin) and, by faith, covering it with Christ's blood.</u>

Our wise Advocate doesn't need to argue against the accuser's lies; He may even agree with them. <u>But, and this is the key: He calls the blood of the Lamb to testify on our behalf.</u> He explains to the Judge that <u>when we received Christ into our hearts, we were covered with the precious blood of the Lamb of God.</u> The blood is our defense and it covers us with the righteousness of God.

<u>So we stand before the Judge as spotless and pure</u> because of Christ's blood. <u>How does the Judge then decide? Not guilty!</u> Then we are no longer bound but free to live in Christ. I believe that's the essence of this concept and the power of the Gospel. Instead of repeating our sins over and over, <u>our confession of faith should line up with the Judge's declaration: Not guilty. Forgiven by the blood of Jesus</u>!

7. Imagine interceding for someone in the courtroom of heaven. How might your prayer sound? Record some key points here.

_____

_____

_____

_____

_____

_____

_____

The importance of soul rest...

There is a verse in Hebrews that at first seems like a mistake, in that it is a paradox that doesn't seem to make sense. ***Hebrews 4:11*** in the Amplified Bible says, ***"Let us therefore be <u>zealous</u> and <u>exert ourselves</u> and <u>strive diligently</u> to enter that <u>rest of God,</u> (to know and experience it for ourselves), that no one may fall or perish by the same kind of unbelief and disobedience into which those in the wilderness fell."*** How can we zealously strive and exert ourselves and be at rest at the same time? Somehow it must be possible, and <u>to not do it implies unbelief or disobedience</u>. So how do we actually enter that rest of God, to really know and experience it? And what happens when we do?

Recently, I've been blessed to use Oswald Chambers, *My Utmost for His Highest*, as one of my daily devotionals. For many years, I could not "get into" that book like I could others, but now the time is right and I'm discovering great treasures of truth. I highly recommend this devotional to anyone serious about the calling to intercession.

I mention this book because all the way through is the answer to the paradox in ***Hebrews 4:11.*** The key to rest is abandonment to God...emptiness of self..."not my will but Thine." We are encouraged to abandon all that we think, feel, and have for the higher purposes of God. As we do this, we come to a place of emptiness, where we almost feel numb to the negatives of this world. It's actually a wonderful place of surrender out of respect for the sovereignty of God. And that, I believe, is the place of rest described in Hebrews.

Perhaps the greatest difficulty of entering into that rest is when we are holding onto promises we believe God has given us, for example promises for healing or salvation. We know that to walk in faith, we must cling to God's Word, confess His truth, and never doubt. Isn't God's covenant of blessing to be true for us? Isn't healing and salvation God's will? This is perhaps the most difficult area for believers to walk in. How do we hold true to faith and yet surrender our will to God's will? Isn't that compromising our faith?

To answer those questions, we look to Jesus who poured out drops of blood in his agony before He was arrested. Did He know truth, that He was the Son of God Himself, that He held the keys to death and life in His hands, that He was the Messiah and conquering King of kings? Of course he knew these truths; that's what made His agony so intense. In the Garden of Gethsemene, Jesus seemed to be facing the opposite of all these truths. He knew he was to face an excruciating death and look like a forsaken failure, anything but the Messiah and conquering King of Kings. He asked in earnest for this cup of suffering to pass...but ultimately He knew that even HE, the Son of God Himself, needed to submit to the perfect sovereignty of the Almighty God, the Father He knew and trusted with all His heart. So with those few poignant words, Jesus said, ***"Nevertheless, not my will but thine be done." (Luke 22:42)*** And all of humanity was given the way of life because of those words.

There's such a fine line between tenaciously believing God in faith and presumptuously holding on to our own will and purposes. But when we reach the point of surrender, feeling like Job must have when he said, ***"Though Thou slay me, yet will I trust You,"*** we know true rest. ***(Job 13:15)***

The place of rest is where the power lies. Our rest frees God to move. It's like all our prayers and tears open the way for His power. Those prayers and tears are necessary and good, but our intercession should not end there. It should lead to a time of utter abandonment to the warm and strong embrace of our Almighty Father God. That's where the victory is won.

What can the enemy do to a heart that is in God's rest? Not a thing. We are untouchable. We are hidden under the shelter of God's wings as described so eloquently in ***Psalm 91.*** That rest is like the eye of a hurricane, the safest and most peaceful place to be. *"For thus said the Lord God, the Holy One of Israel: In returning to Me and resting in Me you shall be saved; in <u>quietness and in (trusting) confidence shall be your strength</u>" Isaiah 30:15*

If truly we believe <u>the battle belongs to the Lord, then perhaps one of our best weapon of warfare is our soul at rest</u>. This is a clear sign to the enemy that he dare not attack there, for the power of God is upon us and all around us.

8.   How have you experienced a time of abandonment to God that brought great rest? In times of crisis?

_____

_____

_____

In ordinary daily activities?

_____

_____

9.   How can you know when you have stepped out of that rest and how do you return?

_____

_____

_____

_____

Approaching the throne of grace…

So in concluding this chapter, let's return to the word "grace." It's a soft comforting word, yet powerful and strengthening. We'd do well to thank God for it each day. And praying in the Spirit both builds up our inner being and releases the grace of God into every situation.

The entire *fourth chapter of Hebrews* gives us valuable keys to triumphing in the battles we face. We can never forget God's word, <u>the Sword of the Spirit being sharper</u> than a two edged sword dividing soul and spirit (*verse 12*). And also remember the fact that we have <u>a High Priest who is</u>

able to understand and sympathize with us completely *(verse 15).* This chapter ends with a strong piece of advice.

We are encouraged to approach the Almighty God and ask for His grace to be released into any and every need. *Hebrews 4:16 says, "Let us then <u>fearlessly and confidently and boldly draw near to the throne of grace</u> (the throne of God's unmerited favor to us sinners), that we may receive mercy (for our failures) and <u>find grace to help</u> in good time for every need (appropriate help and well-timed help, coming just when we need it.)"*

Words that stand out to me are "fearlessly, confidently, and boldly," emphasizing the need to <u>be sure our heart is right with God before we intercede</u>. I also appreciate how the passage mentions the <u>mercy we will no doubt need</u> (assuming we will "blow it" at times) and that grace will come <u>at just the right time and be sufficient</u> for whatever the need is. What a great assurance.

As intercessors, we have the awesome <u>privilege and serious responsibility</u> to come regularly before this throne of grace. It's not like a natural throne room where you must be invited by the king or be on his agenda before you get an audience. The Almighty God gives us an open door to Him where we can come any time. This is the courtroom of heaven where we can gain favor and victory from God for every need.

Moreover, if it is by grace that everything is brought from the kingdom of darkness into the kingdom of light, then as we approach that throne, <u>we can be assured that God's grace is being poured out on the person or need we are interceding for</u>. Of course, we must never forget to believe, for it is also <u>through our faith that grace is best released</u> into the situation.

As we said in the beginning, grace and faith go together. <u>Grace is God's part; faith is ours</u>.

10. Describe a time when you approached the throne of grace for a need and what the outcome was.

_____

_____

_____

_____

_____

_____

Hebrews is an important book for the intercessor. I would encourage you to read and re-read the following verses, to meditate upon them, to study them until they become part of you.

Hebrews 10:19-23 is an incredible reminder in the Amplified Bible: *"Therefore, brethren, since we have <u>full freedom and confidence to enter into the Holy of Holies</u> (by the power and virtue) in <u>the blood of Jesus</u>, by this fresh (new) and living way which He initiated and dedicated and opened for us <u>through the separating curtain</u> (veil of the Holy of Holies), that is through His flesh, and since we have such a great and wonderful and noble Priest (who rules over the house of God,*

Let us all <u>come forward and draw near</u> with true (honest and sincere) hearts in unqualified assurance and <u>absolute conviction engendered by faith</u> (by that leaning of the entire human personality on God in <u>absolute trust and confidence in His power, wisdom, and goodness</u>), having our hearts sprinkled and purified from a guilty (evil) conscience and our bodies cleansed with pure water. So let us <u>seize and hold fast and retain without wavering the hope we cherish and confess and our acknowledgement of it, for He Who promised is reliable (sure) and faithful to His word." Amen. Selah. Never let go of your confidence in the powerful, loving grace of our Lord.

11. After meditating on the verses above, apply them to an intercessory prayer of yours and write out what God would have you say.

_____

_____

_____

_____

_____

_____

Chapter 9:
The Walk of Faith

"Choosing a Different Reality"

What is meant by faith...

Many people talk about their faith, but what does that actually mean? All people have faith in something...maybe science, maybe their own abilities, maybe the gods of other religions. It might even be said that some Christians seem to live with more faith in their past, the world around them, or the devil than they do in the God they claim to serve. I say that based on what is coming out of their mouths, negative words like, "I know I'll just fail or God never lets good things happen to me, and so forth ad nauseum! Our faith is revealed by what we think and say in our unguarded moments and how we choose to live our life . It is the manifestation of what we believe in our hearts, not just our minds. Therefore, our prayer, like David's, might be **Psalm 51:10 "Create in me a clean heart, O God, and renew a right, persevering, and steadfast spirit within in me."**

My purpose here is to describe what the Christian's walk of faith might look like, although each person's journey is unique and changes in different seasons. Faith is defined as "complete trust or confidence in someone or something." Our goal when we are first saved is usually to grow into having absolute trust in God. But how does that happen? By learning through all our life's experiences that Jesus is with us and that our God will see us through.

As we learn to walk in faith, seeing life more from God's perspective than from our own natural point of view, our faith grows and matures. Each day we live, we choose how we perceive life. Does our contentment depend on things going the way we would like? Do we lose our peace and patience when there are hard times or delays? We will always be growing, from one degree of glory to the next until we see Jesus face to face, but as we mature in our faith, we gain more of an eternal perspective. That's what our faith journey is all about.

My hope in the chapter is that you understand more fully God's calling to walk by faith, rather than by sight, and that you will experience the joy that this walk brings to your soul.

The seed of God's faith...

Can we all agree that God would have all people be saved? (See *I Timothy 2:4*.) If that is so, He must give each person a measure of faith that they can express in order to be saved. *Ephesians 2:8* explains *"For it is by free grace (God's unmerited favor) that you are saved (delivered from judgment and made partakers of Christ's salvation through (your) faith. And this (salvation} is not of your-selves (of your own doing, it came not through your own striving), but it is the gift of God. Not because of works (not the fulfillment of the Law's demands), lest any man should boast. (It is not the result of what anyone can possibly do, so no one can pride himself in it or take glory to himself.) "* That's how our Christian lives began. God poured out saving grace, and we responded with the measure of faith He gave us in order to receive that free gift.

Hebrews 12:2 explains how Jesus is the Source and Finisher of our faith. Other religions always involve striving and works. That's why most of us say we don't have a religion but rather a relation-ship. Do you see how our Christian faith is so different from all other types of faith? Only this faith depends on the grace of the Almighty God, above all else, and that's how we walk in faith.

Once we are saved by grace through our faith, God begins to develop that seed of faith that has been planted in our souls. When we are born of His Spirit, our spirits are completely filled with all that God is. The challenge is that are soul (our mind, will, and emotions) are not instantly saved. We are constantly being challenged to exercise the faith God deposited in us so that we might see that life grow in us. I always think of a seed being planted in our hearts that grows and grows until it (with all its branches) completely takes over our soul.

1. Explain when and how you were saved. Can you see the combination of God's grace and your faith?

    _____

    _____

    _____

Growing in faith...

Jesus explained to His disciples why their prayers weren't enough: *"Because of the littleness of your faith (that is, your lack of firmly relying trust). For truly I say to you, if you have faith (that is living) like a grain of mustard seed, you can say to this mountain, Move from here to yonder place, and it will move; and nothing will be impossible to you." Matthew 17:20* If we have faith, why then are not all the mountains of difficulties in our lives removed? That's a tough question to ask God. Perhaps it's a matter of timing or of God's higher ways, but if we keep our hearts right, He will eventually reveal what we need to know. In all our intercession, we are to <u>balance our prayers of faith with our surrender to the sovereignty of God.</u>

I love the word of the Lord to Zerubbabel in ***Zechariah 4:6-7*** *"Not by might, nor by power, but by My Spirit, says the Lord of hosts.* <u>***This mountain (of human obstacles)…shall become a plain (a mere molehill)!…with shouts of the people, crying Grace, grace to it.***</u>*"* We cannot move mountains; that's God's work. Our responsibility is to feed our faith with the Word of God and to grow in our trust that God knows what He's doing. ***"So*** <u>***faith comes by hearing***</u> ***(what is told), and what is heard comes by the preaching (of the message that came from the lips) of Christ (the Messiah Himself). "*** *Romans 10:17* The Christian journey, therefore, means that we become more like Jesus as our faith grows. ***"And all of us, as with unveiled face, (because we) continued to behold (in the Word of God) as in a mirror the glory of the Lord, are*** <u>***constantly being transfigured into His very own image***</u> ***in every increasing splendor and from one degree of glory to another; (for this comes) from the Lord (Who is) the Spirit."*** *II Corinthians 3:18* Our Christian faith may begin as a seed, but it grows and matures during our lives as we lean on His Word and His Spirit so that the Kingdom of God can be established on the Earth.

2. What is God saying to you today about your faith?

_____

_____

_____

Is seeing believing or is believing seeing?…

The Bible mentions the gifts of the Spirit, which are special manifestations of the Holy Spirit for the good of the body of Christ. Paul explains this in ***Romans 12*** and states in ***verse 9*** *"To another* <u>***(wonder-working) faith***</u> *by the same (Holy) Spirit, to another the extraordinary powers of healing by the one Spirit;"* This is not the faith given to each of us when we are saved, but rather a special impartation of the Spirit for God's purposes or will to be done.

<u>The faith all believers are given is the ability to believe or trust with their whole heart what God says is true.</u> It is not just mentally believing, but knowing deep down, that something is an absolute fact, no matter what circumstances look like. ***Hebrews 11:1 says: "Now faith is the assurance (the confirmation,*** <u>***the title deed)***</u> ***of the things we hope for, being*** <u>***the proof of things***</u> ***we do not see and the conviction of their reality (faith perceiving as real fact what is*** <u>***not revealed to the senses.***</u>***"*** Let's look at this verse a minute. Before moving into a new home, the <u>owner is given the *title deed*,</u> a legal document, to the property. Living in the home may not yet be a reality, but it is a *promise* that can be counted on. Your faith is the *confirmation or assurance* of what has been hoped for. When you

plan a big event, you know a <u>confirmation is necessary</u>, and that's what faith gives you. Not only that, but you begin to be able to imagine and *know the reality* of what has been promised even before you see it manifested in a physical way.

If walking in faith means living in <u>a realm other than what we see, feel, hear, taste, or touch, we are to walk in another reality.</u> Remember what Jesus said to doubting Thomas? ***John 20:29 "Because you have seen Me, Thomas, do you now believe (trust, have faith)? <u>Blessed and happy and to be envied are those who have never seen Me and yet have believed</u> and adhered to and trusted and relied on Me."*** That's the reality we live in when we choose to walk in faith.

3. Describe what you are holding onto by faith, even though you have not seen it manifested.

_____

_____

_____

Protecting that seed of faith...

When God plants seeds of faith in our heart, <u>He expects us to nurture and care for those seeds</u>, like we would a newborn child. We all know what to do to care for a baby, but the same is true for our faith. <u>It takes time and energy to nurture a baby</u>. Just as we might cherish a child and protect him or her with all our might, so must we recognize and <u>take care of this priceless gift</u>, our faith, which God has planted in our hearts. We all want our children to grow and mature, and that should also be our attitude about our faith. C.H. Spurgeon said "Oh brethren, be great believers! Little faith will bring your souls to heaven, but great <u>faith will bring heaven to your souls</u>."

In April, 1999, God told me to <u>protect my faith as I would protect my precious child</u> so I wrote a poem. We all hear of the fury of the mother bear...most of us would do anything to protect our children, but God would have us think the same way about our faith. Although I had my daughter in mind as I wrote this, as you read it, remember it's a description of the treasure of our faith in Christ.

The Greatest Treasure

My faith is so much like my natural daughter—
A special gift, a treasure to fill my heart.
I remember when she was first given to me,
Small and fragile, God's promise from the start,
Life was in her, a depth of life I'd never known,
I held her close and embraced her as my own.

As the years passed, I saw her growing—
Oddly, the more I suffered, the more she grew.
There were times I almost forgot her,
So wrapped in the pain and struggles I knew.
But she remained shining brightly throughout the dark
Like an anchor for my soul to hold me to the mark.

Then came the day when her maturity would blossom,
Hardships we shared transforming into treasure.
It seemed evident that somehow I'd done something right,
Or perhaps it was all her Father's good pleasure—
For He had always been faithful to meet her need,
Protecting and nurturing the precious life of His seed.

Now looking back, she's my greatest gift ever,
One I should nourish and guard with my being,
Dearer than life—or is she my life?—
Always mine, her beauty worth seeing,
Nothing can take her from me, for we're one,
This priceless gift from Father and Son—
I treasure my faith.

Proverbs 4:23 "Keep and guard your heart with all vigilance and above all that you guard, for out of it flow the spring of life."

4. Explain or describe the seed of faith that God has planted in your heart.

_____

_____

_____

How has that seed been tested during your life?

_____

_____

_____

How have you learned to protect, nurture, and develop that seed?

_____

_____

_____

It's a marathon, not a sprint...

The walk of faith might best be described in **Hebrews 12:1-2.** *"Therefore then, since we are surrounded by so great a cloud of witnesses (who have borne testimony to the Truth), <u>let us strip off and throw aside every encumbrance</u> (unnecessary weight) and that sin which so readily (deftly and cleverly) clings to and entangles us, and <u>let us run with patient endurance</u> and steady and active persistence the appointed course of the race that is set before us, <u>looking away (from all that will distract) to Jesus</u>..."* When we picture a marathon, we always see crowds looking on; I believe these are heroes of faith and loved ones in heaven who are still cheering us on. Runners strip down to the bare essentials, and so we too must get rid of all that hinders our walk of faith. Endurance and persistence will also be required, as we keep our focus on Jesus, the Author and Finisher of our faith.

Our faith is secure, protected by the Spirit Himself, but life can bring some severe happenings that will test or faith. We might even forget we have that seed of faith for a time, but God never does. God <u>always looks at our hearts instead of our deeds and stays with us</u> throughout our journey of faith. **Matthew 28:20 *"I am with you all the days (perpetually, uniformly, and on every occasion), to the (very) close and consummation of the Age."***

I personally believe that once we are truly saved and the Spirit of God joins with our spirits, we can never become "unsaved." I know this is debated often by Christians, and I won't try to convince you of my viewpoint. Let me just say that if God does not condone abortion, <u>how could He ever abort new life that has been planted in any true believer's heart</u>? We may seem to completely abandon our Christian faith, but that's why Jesus gave us the beautiful redemptive story of the prodigal son.

(Luke 15:11-32) Let us remember and cling to <u>this hope as we pray for our wayward children</u> or other prodigals, looking at them always with eyes of faith and hearts of love.

Matthew 7:13-14 explains that there is a wide way to destruction and a narrow way to life. How much easier our lives would be if we were never led astray with detours during our faith journey? But as we will see, even then God is with us. In *John 10:27-29* Jesus explains how the shepherd will even leave 99 of his sheep to look for the one who went astray. <u>The cord of God's love is always attached to the wayward child of His.</u>

Many of us, however, stay on the "straight and narrow" for the most part, but we may just be plodding along that path, with little joy and maybe even frustration and disappointment. It shouldn't always be like that. Jesus said He gives us the promise of abundant life *(John 10:10)*, and that includes an <u>abundance of joy and peace.</u> May God give each of us a greater revelation about what it means <u>to live with a deep and true faith that provides us an abundant and free life.</u>

Our Lord is a Gentleman; He never forces His way on His people. But, like any good parent, He wants us all to grow and prosper. *3 John 1:2* reveals the Father's heart: ***"Beloved, <u>I pray that you may prosper</u> in every way and (that your body) may keep well, even as (I know) your soul keeps well and prospers."*** We choose daily if we want our lives to mature this way. We can act like we have faith when we pray, reciting God's promises and praying religiously, but without faith it accomplishes little. Remember Jesus' words in *Matthew 15:8* about the Pharisees ***"These people draw near Me with their mouths and honor Me with their lips, but <u>their hearts hold off and are far away from Me</u>."***

We never want our words to be empty repetitions; that's why we ask God to search our hearts and even give us the faith to pray as He would. When God gives us faith for something, we feel the difference, and our prayers are full of the power of God Himself.

5. What have you learned to strip off while you are on your faith marathon?

_____

_____

_____

_____

The role of hope...

I think we begin to exercise our faith by believing God will do something for us, and He often does. However, many are disappointed in their walk of faith when prayers are not answered as they hoped. It's so easy to focus on the *answer* to prayer rather than the *Answer Himself*, to focus on what God *does* or *doesn't do* more than on Who He *is*, on His *hand* instead of on His *face*. When we <u>focus more on the *Father's faithfulness*</u> than on our own faith, we are not disappointed.

As we learn to walk in faith, we may face numerous obstacles, but God will never allow more than we can endure ***"But God is faithful (to His Word and to His compassionate nature), and He can be trusted) <u>not to let you be tempted and tried and assayed beyond your ability and strength of resistance and power to endure</u>, but with the temptation He will (always) <u>provide the way out</u>...that you may be capable and strong and powerful to bear up under it patiently." I Corinthians 10:13***

For faith to survive and even flourish, there must be hope. *Hope is the expectancy that God will be faithful because He is always good.* <u>When we hope, we are expecting to see the goodness of the Lord in our life's circumstances.</u> ***Psalm 27:13-14 "(What, what would have become of me) <u>had I not believed that I would see the Lord's goodness</u> in the land of the living! Wait and hope for and expect the Lord; be brave and of good courage and let your heart be stout and enduring. <u>Yes, wait for and hope for and expect the Lord.</u>"***

Years ago I came to understand the connection between hope and faith. I saw in my mind a campfire that had burned out, looking dead. God was showing me that although the flames were gone, live coals remained that were able to once again ignite the fire. <u>Hope is like these coals or embers</u>. Hope can be fanned to ignite new material that would <u>then burst into large flames</u>. The flames are the fire of our faith. We don't need to wait until we feel great faith when we pray. We can fan the coals of hope with the breath of the Spirit, and our faith will arise.

Here is my prayer for you, ***"May the <u>God of your hope so fill you with all joy and peace in believing</u> (through the experience of your faith) that by the power of the Holy Spirit you may abound and be overflowing <u>(bubbling over) with hope</u>." Romans 15:14*** May we each become ambassadors of hope, spreading words of hope to everyone we know.

6. What do you hope for?

   _____

   _____

   How can that hope ignite your faith?

   _____

   _____

What might you do to stir up your faith when you don't see prayers answered?

_____

_____

_____

The path to despair...

The opposite of hope is despair. <u>Experiencing despair is like pouring water over burning coals.</u> It is the complete loss or absence of hope. *Proverbs 13:12* says *"Hope deferred makes the heart sick, but when the desire is fulfilled it is a tree of life."* When hope is deferred, we benefit from a serious talk with ourselves. David understood this and wrote: *"<u>Why are you cast down, O my inner self?</u> And why should you moan over me and be disquieted within me? <u>Hope in God and wait expectantly for Him,</u> for I shall yet praise Him, Who is the help of my (sad) countenance, and my God." Psalm 43:5*

Despair doesn't just happen. <u>It is a dark road that begins with disappointment, leading to discouragement and depression.</u> This is a dangerous and destructive path, and we should learn to depart from it at the outset. *I Peter 5:8-9* advises us of our enemy's tactics to seize upon and devour. *"<u>Withstand him; be firm in faith</u> (against his onset—rooted, established, strong, immovable, and determined), knowing that the same (identical) sufferings are appointed to your brotherhood (the whole body of Christians) throughout the world."* Our positive declaration of faith is needed here.

How often do we hear or even say, "I don't want to get my hopes up," but that's exactly what we should do in our faith walk. Why not? <u>If we hold onto hope, we may enjoy life more, and live in more victory.</u> We have nothing to lose and everything to gain. <u>Hope must be kept alive,</u> even when the desired outcome is delayed. We need to <u>stir up hope in others and in ourselves.</u> Our circumstances, our own thinking, or the devil would like to quench our hope.

We must not let that happen because hope is needed to ignite our faith, and it is our faith that enables us to triumph. *I John 5:4 "For whatever is born of God is victorious over the world; and <u>this is the victory that conquers the world, even our faith.</u>"* That's why the enemy of our souls hates our faith more than anything. He knows that if he can distract us from believing and walking in faith or if he can cause us to lose our hope or wear us out in our prayers, then he will handicap our lives and hinder the purposes of God on the earth. Paul wrote in *II Corinthians 4:8, "We are hedged in (pressed) on every side (troubled and oppressed in every way), but not cramped or crushed; we suffer embarrassments and are perplexed and unable to find a way out, <u>but not driven to despair.</u>"* If early disciples never gave up their hope, we should be able to hold onto hope also while on our marathon of faith.

Hebrews 6:19 "(Now) <u>we have this hope as a sure and steadfast anchor of the soul</u> (It cannot slip and it cannot break down under whoever steps out upon it—a hope) that reaches farther and enters into (the very certainty of the Presence) within the veil." Hope will anchor you to Jesus.

Over the years I've seen many prayers answered and others not. How do we explain these happenings? Did we lack faith or fail in our intercession…why wasn't that child healed…why wasn't that marriage restored? When we pray according to God's will as written in the Word, shouldn't our prayers be answered that way? <u>That's our human reasoning, but we are called to a higher way</u>. When we begin to feel discouraged, we do well to <u>shift our prayers to praise and thanksgiving</u>. We also might <u>reflect on God's great faithfulness to us in the past</u>. May favorite hymn is "Great is Thy Faithfulness" and those lyrics may stir up hope in our hearts.

7. When has your hope wavered and what did you do to stir it up?

_____

_____

_____

_____

_____

_____

I still wonder about this at times, but my conclusion is simple: "God is always <u>good</u> and <u>loving,</u> and He is <u>sovereign</u>." We may suffer disillusionment, discouragement, or even despair after intense intercession that seems to have failed. But as it says in *Isaiah 55:8, "My thoughts are not your thoughts, neither are your ways My ways, says the Lord."* <u>We may not understand until we see God face to face</u>, but we can know and trust that He will see us through every difficulty and that He will ALWAYS *work together ALL things for good for those who are called according to His purposes (Romans 8:28).*

My faith or God's faithfulness…

Proverbs 3:5-6 advises us, "Trust in the Lord with all your heart and lean on your own understanding. In all your ways acknowledge Him and He will direct your paths." Oswald Chambers explains how our <u>faith may actually be misplaced if we lean on our own understanding</u>. He states in *My Utmost for His Highest,* "My misgivings arise from the fact that <u>I ransack my own person to find out how He will be able to do it.</u> My questions spring from the depths of my own inferiority. If I detect these misgivings in myself, let me bring them to the light and confess them—'Lord, I have had misgivings about Thee, I have not believed in Thy wits apart from my own; I have not believed in Thy almighty power apart from my finite understanding if it.'"

Perhaps we may get disappointed because we misplaced our faith, putting faith more in what we want to happen than in getting to know God more deeply. Our faith should always be in our God Himself, in His faithful character, not in what He is able to do. Our attention may begin to focus so much on the need and how we feel it should be resolved, that we are disappointed when things don't work out as we believed. Sometimes we may actually *believe more in our beliefs or have faith more in our faith,* than in God Himself.

A good reminder about intercession is ***Psalm 37:3-5 "Trust (lean on, rely on, and be confident) in the Lord and do good; so shall you dwell in the land and feed surely on His faithfulness, and truly you shall be fed. Delight yourself also in the Lord, and He will give you the desires and secret petitions of your hear. Commit your way to the Lord (roll and repose each care of your loan on Him); trust (lean on, rely on and be confident) also in Him and He will bring it to pass."*** Trust. delight, commit. Once the need has been committed to the Lord, through our bringing it to the cross and expecting God's redemptive power to be released, it may be time for our prayers to be changed into *praise and thanksgiving.* God knows more about the situation than we do, so we don't need to continually re-explain, direct, prescribe, or plead with Him. Our time would be better spent focusing on who He is, our Omniscient, Omnipotent Lord, and thanking Him for His great love for us and His constant faithfulness.

As we mature in our faith, we begin to focus more on God's faithfulness than we do on our faith. We use our faith to cry out to God, but our focus remains on His great faithfulness, no matter what happens or doesn't happen. That's how we walk in faith…with our eyes on His faithfulness. Even when we find that walk to be difficult, we can trust in Him. ***"It is because of the Lord's mercy and loving-kindness that we are not consumed, because His (tender) compassions fail not. They are new every morning: great and abundant is Your stability and faithfulness."*** *Lamentations 3:22-23*

8. Explain one time when you were disappointed in a time of prayer?

_____

_____

What are your thoughts on this now?

_____

_____

_____

The posture of faith...

Sometimes the battles of life are so great or so prolonged, that we grow weary and feel we could faint. ***"And <u>let us not lose heart and grow weary and faint</u> in acting nobly and doing right, for in due time and at the appointed season we shall reap, if we do not loosen and relax our courage and faint." Galatians 6:9*** In the marathon of walking in faith, we often need a third, fourth, or hundredth "second wind." Draw near to God, and He will refresh you and renew your faith. It is at these times especially we must remember that the battle belongs to the Lord and that the war has already been won. <u>Our role as His soldier is to show up on the battlefield, to take our positions, to raise our banners of faith, and to move as He directs.</u>

Chuck Pierce, in his excellent book, *The Shield of Our Faith*, explains that the ancient Roman shields actually linked together, so that a row of soldiers raising their shields would create a solid, impenetrable barrier to the enemy's blows. What a great picture to remind us of <u>our need for linking our faith and prayers with others in the body of Christ</u>. Our enemy's battle strategy, however, is sometimes to isolate us. As the battles intensify, we dare not try to stand alone.

Another passage ***(Exodus 17:12)*** that illustrates our posture during a battle is when Moses was growing weary of the battle and <u>he called on Aaron and Hur to each lift up one of his arms</u>. When Moses' arms were raised, God's armies were victorious; if they were lowered, they met defeat. What a great picture to remind us of our need for others to come alongside us and support us in our faith. It also illustrates the posture we must be careful to maintain: our arms lifted in *praise and worship* to the Almighty King.

The enemy of our souls strives to wear us out when the battle rages. He throws darts at our shield of faith constantly. We must remain girded with all the spiritual armor God has given us to use. As explained in ***Ephesians 6:10-18***, I believe with His *helmet of salvation* on, our minds are constantly protected by the powerful blood He shed for our salvation, our healing, and our deliverance. With His *breastplate of righteousness,* our hearts are secure and guarded because it is His goodness and worthiness alone that brings us the victory. With His *belt of Truth* at the center of our being, all our armor stays in place. With the *Gospel of peace* on our feet, we are ready to advance, maintain our ground, and even retreat when necessary because we are at rest in the midst of turmoil, having learned to abide in His secret place daily. <u>And with the *sword of God's authoritative Word*, we not only can defend ourselves, but we can take an offensive position, ready to attack the enemy forces and disarm his lies and foil his strategies.</u> God has prepared us well, if we only remember to put on that full armor daily.

This is the posture or preparation we must have to survive as intercessors. We dare not wear "Saul's armor," thinking that the world or its wisdom has solutions to our problems. Remember when David went to face Goliath, he rejected wearing Saul's armor and went out instead as he was ***"in the name of the Lord of Hosts." (*** See ***I Samuel 17:39, 45.)*** We must daily remember that only God supplies what is just right for each of us. And only God can give us the right stones and show us how to strike a fatal blow on the giant that confronts us.

9. When was a time when you knew your posture in a certain battle was key to your victory?

_____

_____

_____

What should you remember the next time the battle rages around you and you feel weary or overwhelmed?

_____

_____

_____

Aligning ourselves in faith...

Clearly the issue of faith could (and does) fill volumes of books, and I highly recommend Chuck Pierce's book that I referred to earlier. My hope in this chapter is just to <u>remind us that when God doesn't *seem* to be working in a situation, it does not mean He *isn't*</u>. He's just testing our faith to see what's really in our hearts. He knows our faith is eternal and that we will be greatly rewarded for how we've used our faith when we meet Him face to face.

Sometimes we may feel our prayers are not working. Here's a great promise to hold onto (and to flaunt in the enemy's face) as well as a provocative challenge. It is ***Luke 18:7-8: "And will not <u>our just God defend and protect and avenge His elect</u>** (His chosen ones), **who cry to Him day and night? Will He defer them and delay help on their behalf? I tell you, <u>He will defend and protect and avenge them speedily.</u>"** But then Jesus questions, **"However, <u>when the Son of Man comes, will He find persistence in faith on the earth</u>?"***

The big question is not what God will do, but rather how will the Lord find our faith when he returns? All through the Gospels, Jesus rebuked His followers saying, ***"Oh, ye of little faith."*** And remember that He could do no miracles in places because of their unbelief. So faith is obviously critical to our prayers and ***"without faith it is impossible to please God." (Hebrews 11:6)***

Unfortunately when we hear this appeal for greater faith, we often assume it means we have to try harder to have more faith. This self-effort or "works" is not in the nature of the Gospel. Our good works must be the *result* or by-product of our life of faith, not the *cause* of it. If it is *by grace* we are saved through faith, then it is *by grace through our faith* that we are able to grow as Christians; *Philippians 2:12 -13* advises ***"work our (cultivate, carry out to the goal, and fully complete) your own salvation** with reverence and awe and trembling (self-distrust, with serious caution, tenderness of conscience, watchfulness against temptation, timidly shrinking from whatever might offend God and discredit the name of Christ) (not **in your own strength) for it is God Who is all the while effectually at work in you (energizing and creating in you the power and desire) both to will and to work for His good pleasure and satisfaction and delight.***" So again, it's all about God's great grace given to us.

It is not our strenuous effort to grow in faith that we need to show, but rather it's a matter of *aligning ourselves with what Jesus has already done.* If we remember that He paid the price for it all and believe that truth in our inmost being, we are properly aligning our faith. Without this type of faith it is impossible to please God, but with true faith, all things are possible. Let's remember that faith cannot be conjured up through vain repetitions or even positive confessions. Faith is the product of the grace of God being extended to us. God does the work (or rather has already done the work). We have only to align ourselves from the inside out with His victory. That is the faith that endures long periods in the wilderness. That is the faith that revives the weary and downtrodden. And that is the faith that overcomes all of life's challenges, that overcomes the world!

Christ died not only to restore us to fellowship with Father God, but to bring us into victorious daily living, overcoming any and every obstacle. As Jesus reminded us, ***"Fear not, for I have overcome the world." (John 16:33.)*** Since He indeed has overcome it, He can enable us to overcome the ways and thoughts of the world also. When we live in this faith, we abide in the power of the Gospel. The truth is *we* can never overcome the world or our circumstances. Only God can, and through Jesus' sacrifice, He already has. So we return to the simple truth. It's not about us; it's all about God. Our job is to align ourselves (through our faith) with Jesus, the great High Priest, and watch what He can do through us. That way, only He gets the glory, for only He is worthy. Amen? Amen!

10. Write a declaration of faith here.

_____

_____

_____

_____

Now write a three-step plan for abiding in faith while you intercede for others. This is a "to do list" of such things as these: Focus on God instead of the problem. Turn every negative thought into a positive Truth from God's Word...etc.

_____

_____

_____

In conclusion, here are two acronyms based on the letters of Hope and Faith.

Holding	**F** – Focus on Jesus.	Focusing
Onto	**A**– Always give thanks.	**All**
Promises	**I** – Imagine the unseen.	Imagination
Evermore	**T** – Trust in His love.	Toward
	H – Hold fast to your hope.	Hope

11. Write your own acronyms here:

H– _____   F – _____

O – _____   A – _____

P – _____   I – _____

E– _____   T– _____

                                         H– _____

Habakkuk 2:4b says "the (rigidly) just and the (uncompromisingly) righteous man shall live by his faith and in his faithfulness."

Chapter 10:
Where Faith Takes Us

"Journeying to the High Places"

Redefining identity...

In order to live a successful Christian life, <u>we not only need to know who God is but who we are in Christ.</u> *"Therefore if any person is (ingrafted) in Christ (the Messiah) he is a new creation (a new creature altogether); the old (previous moral and spiritual condition) has passed away. Behold, the fresh and new has come!" (II Corinthians 5:17).* Some people go through a dramatic and instant change, others grow into their new identity slowly as they walk by faith, and some experience little outward change although their spirit has already become new. Why such differences? <u>Perhaps it depends on how deeply they seek to understand their new identity.</u> Knowing who we are in Christ is essential to our growth as Christians. The truth of who we are in Christ <u>takes our intentional thoughts and deepening understanding of His Word.</u> As we walk by faith, we see new facets of our identity develop as we become more like Christ.

The first 25 years of my Christian life, I worked in ministry organizations where I was able to learn and grow, coming to know who I was in Christ. I received deep teaching and wonderful support from my brothers and sisters in the Lord. However, <u>the Lord knew my identity in Him was not yet completely formed.</u>

After completing fourteen years in Christian education and ten years working in international ministry, I left the security of that work to be "sent into the field." I moved into my childhood home close to the city of Seattle and took a teaching job with the public school system. Here I was, returning to the area of my childhood, to where I was before I knew the Lord. I had become a new creation, but my identity had been mostly in Christian circles. Now my life became very different, and <u>I experienced a type of identity crisis.</u>

The first year I was there, I went through a type of culture shock, feeling like I was losing the identity I had known for many years and being stretched into new horizons. I busied myself with many things, not directly connected to the Lord. One day during my long commute to south Seattle, I found myself remembering my previous life and feeling I had become a different person. I determined that day to <u>reawaken the spiritual identity that I had previously known.</u>

This was a season of deep inner reflection for me...<u>Who was I really? What did I believe with all my heart</u>? What was God's purpose for me during this season? Little by little I began to rediscover my true identity, a richer identity, and to enjoy the fellowship with the Lord that I had been missing. I began to rekindle the flames of faith that had once burned brightly in me. This was <u>the beginning of connecting more fully to a multi-cultured field</u>, to a world that needed to know the love of God. I believe that this connection was an act of intercession. As I reflect back on those years, I appreciate how God expanded my heart to so many different people. Although I couldn't preach the Gospel in a public school, I could be salt and light in that place. But that wasn't so easy. It never is when God is doing a deep work in us.

1. Describe who you are in Christ.

    _____

    _____

    Have you ever seen your identity expanded or changed?

    _____

    _____

On eagles' wings...

As I reflect on my past now, I see <u>how God's hand has gently led me into different places</u>, different roles, and different jobs. My next public school teaching job was in the center of Seattle, right next to the Space Needle, where I had often prayed with teams for my city.

The first few days the school was open, we experienced the tragedy of 9/11, and I observed how some at the heart of my hometown reacted. Although all experienced shock and grief, there wasn't any prayer in this setting; no one spoke in terms of hope or faith. Over the seven years I taught there, the gap between me and others in that school widened. I felt very alone with my contrary life philosophy and my godly belief system. This was another challenge for me...Could I accept where God had placed me, appreciate how God was enriching my identity and let Him lead me to explore how to serve Him? <u>It was a stretching time of growth in knowing my identity in Christ.</u>

I knew God loved the city of my birth, and that He has had His eye on Seattle. Over the years, some powerful spiritual movements were birthed in this city. Great works of the Lord had happened here, and it has been the focus of much prayer for decades. However, now I was seeing a different reality, working with many who were far from the Lord. I began to learn how God indeed loved this place and was having mercy on its people. So these years of living in the <u>cultural heart of the city and getting to know her even better brought me into a season of creative intercession</u>.

Interestingly, one day I saw an article on the front page of our local *Times Newspaper* with this headline, "The Eagles Go to the Urban Places." Why had these birds begun to inhabit the urban places? How strange was that? Knowing that God's prophets and intercessors were sometimes referred to as eagles, and that my last name was the action word for eagle in Spanish, I began to wonder what God might be saying to me. Here I was, a country-girl at heart, spending day after day in the concrete world of Seattle. So I identified with these urban eagles.

"How do eagles survive in the city?" I pondered from time to time. "They'd have nothing to eat. No lakes to swoop down to. No trees to find refreshment in. They must return to the country to eat and be refreshed," I concluded. And so it was for me, that I began to see how my quiet times with the Lord were to be critical to my "survival" during this season. Eagles are solitary birds. They soar on the wind, not needing to flap their wings. They perch high above the land on the tops of trees; and with keen vision, they can swoop down in an instant when they spot prey from miles away. They can see at night, and their eyes see forward and to the side simultaneously. They are incredible creatures, but I wondered how I could ever be like that in my urban place. My prayer was and still is: May God give us eagle eyes to see our circumstances from His perspective. *Isaiah 40:31 "But those who __wait for the Lord__ (who expect, look for, and hope in Him) shall change and renew their strength and power; __they shall lift their wings and mount up (close to God) as eagles__ (mount up close to the sun); they shall run and not be weary, they shall walk and not faint or become tired."*

2. Think about what you know about eagles. Can you see why an eagle may represent the prophet or the intercessor?

_____

_____

_____

> **My hope in this chapter is that you will know who you are in Christ at this point in your journey and that you will be strengthened to press into all that God has called you to be and to go joyfully where He would take you..**

For such a time as this...

While I was still at the Center School, I had a strange dream one night. Since the school was affiliated with the Arts and Theater, in my dream the entire staff was sitting around a large boardroom table, planning some dramatic production. I was behind everyone with two slips of paper in my hands. I began walking around the table, pondering the part I was to play in the upcoming drama. When

I nearly finished circling the table, I looked at my paper and said to myself, "Queen Esther? I can't play the part of Queen Esther. I could never memorize all those lines." Then I woke up. I never saw what was on the other paper, but I wondered but God wanted to tell me about Queen Esther and the role I was to play.

During those years, I began to hear other prophetic voices speaking about the Queen Esther calling to intercede for others. God was urging many to come before His throne and speak to Him in favor of His people "for such a time as this." *Esther 4:14 "For if you keep silent at this time, relief and deliverance shall arise from the Jews from elsewhere, but you and your father's house will perish. And who knows but that you have come to the kingdom for such a time as this and for this very occasion?"* The lives of God's people depended upon Esther's intercession. I began to press into God about what I should bring before the King.

I pondered these thoughts for a few years until 2008 when God led me to another school where I began to teach English to students from many different countries. The five years spent at that school taught me many additional lessons about God's heart for all people, and stretched my intercessory muscles in even more ways. And when I finally left the public school system, it was with a sincere appreciation for all the types of people God had brought into my life. I could see God's love for them...I had come to see beyond their ways and words and into their hearts. Those years were essential to making me the intercessor God is calling me to be, and someday I may know even more about why I was there.

3. Can you explain a time when you knew you were called to a certain situation "for such a time as this?

_____

_____

_____

Tunnel times...

The years I spent away from ministry, in the public school system, were in many ways my tunnel years. Times in the wilderness or tunnel times are difficult and meant to strengthen us. They are times when our faith is tested, purified, tried and refined that it might come forth as pure as gold. I remember hearing that the refiner of precious metals will heat up the fire under the metals until he is able to see his reflection in the liquid. Think of Job's dark days, not because of his sin, but to bring God greater glory. *Job 23:10 "But He knows the way that I take (He has concern for it, appreciates, and pays attention to it). When He has tried me, I shall come forth as refined gold (pure and luminous)."*

Many years ago I travelled with my parents through Norway. My father decided to cross from west to east through the mountains. So for hours, we went through tunnel after tunnel. The <u>longest tunnel we drove through was seven miles long</u>. I did not enjoy those minutes. It was dark. I felt so alone and vulnerable. What if??? I couldn't imagine having car trouble or an accident while in that tunnel... being trapped in that dark place. But oh, the relief when we made it through! Once again we could freely drive in the open air. <u>That's a picture of what it's like during some seasons of our Christian lives</u>. They are not enjoyable...and may be quite dark...but they are getting us somewhere. That's what tunnel times are like.

<u>What tunnels did I go through for seven years, 2003-2010</u>? For me those years meant working at a place where my values and beliefs were not appreciated or tolerated, going through the rejection of a divorce, caring for my dear elderly mother who lived with me and suffered from Alzheimer's disease, suffering the unimaginable brutal murder of my beloved brother, and investing many resources into a home for my only daughter and her family that would then be lost to a bank in foreclosure.

However, <u>there was always hope and encouragement from the Lord</u> during those years.

I was able to purchase a piece of waterfront land that I felt was meant to be "a light at the end of the tunnel." This beautiful lake lot gave me hope. That was in 2003 and as we went through various difficulties, God was faithful. In 2010 interestingly enough, because of the world's economic crisis, I had to give up my lake lot to the bank. It was a very difficult time of injustice and foreclosure of properties by banks. However, rather than seeing the loss of our home and this land as stolen by the enemy, <u>I began to realize that they had been temporary blessings, now to remain as a monument of "my surrender to the goodness of the Lord,</u>" because God had better plans. <u>It's always about perspective</u>, how we learn to see life's challenges, from God's viewpoint, not ours. God knew I'd no longer need that light to keep me moving through the long seven-year tunnel. <u>God had intervened</u> and brought my family safely to the other end of the tunnel, to a broad and beautiful property which met my family's needs perfectly.

During those years <u>I felt like I was in a tunnel...restricted but moving forward</u>. I was only able to endure the trials and difficulties by leaning on the Lord and taking one more step forward, grace upon grace. "One day at a time" was a poem I wrote then. Maybe this is good advice for all of us as we continue on our journey of faith.

One Day at a Time (March, 2006)

One day at a time, Lord, One day at a time.
That's all I will take, Lord, That's all that is mine.

Someday I will know, Lord, how it all works for good.
Someday I will see, Lord, how well my faith stood.

One day at a time, Lord, I'll walk by Your side.
One day at a time, Lord, You'll be my sweet Guide.

You'll keep and protect us, and lead us each day.
You'll comfort and cheer us, and show us the way.

One day at a time, Lord, I'll rest in your care.
One day at a time, Lord. I know You are there.

I know you are faithful; as You've been, You will be.
Your love can't be broken; Your grace strong and free.

Joshua 1:9 "Have not I commanded you? <u>Be strong, vigorous, and very courageous</u>. Be not afraid, neither be dismayed, for <u>the Lord your God is with you wherever you go</u>."

4. What have you learned about tunnel times? What keeps you going?

_____

_____

_____

When God is nowhere to be seen...

Toward the end of my tunnel years, I became part of a Bible study on Queen Esther at a nearby church in Seattle. I expected to learn in that study why God had given me that dream about playing the role of Queen Esther, but what stood out to me most, I heard the first night of the study. **Esther is the only book in the Bible where God is not directly mentioned**.

Indeed, the book of <u>Esther is a story about a tunnel time</u>...a dark time with no way of escape...<u>but a time to trust that the invisible God was truly there and able to bring forth the deliverance of His people</u>. Esther had no idea why she had become queen, and later did not feel equipped for the challenge she faced... but there she was. <u>She had no choice but to trust and obey</u>. Was it by chance she was queen, or did God choose her because He knew her heart of faith? Was her position the working of a sovereign God for a purpose that at first was unknown to her? Praise God, we know how Esther's story ends; God is always victorious.

After Jesus was crucified and resurrected, two disciples were walking on the way to Emmaus, discussing what had just happened. It must have seemed like a tunnel time to them. As they discussed their disappointment with a fellow traveler, they had no idea it was Jesus Himself actually walking with them. When He opened their eyes to see Him, they rejoiced at all He shared with them. *(See Luke 24:13-33.)* When we are in a dark time, Jesus is walking with us, speaking encouragement to our hearts, even when we may not recognize Him.

Remember also Jesus' words to "doubting Thomas" in ***John 20:29 "Jesus said to him, 'Because you have seen Me, Thomas, do you now believe (trust, have faith)? Blessed and <u>happy and to be envied are those who have never seen Me and yet have believed</u> and adhered to and trusted and relied on Me.'"***

5. Describe a time when you wondered if Jesus was near to you? How did your faith help you through that time?

_____

_____

_____

Our confession of faith...

We may not know where our walk of faith will take us; <u>the journey is far more important than the destination</u>. How will we journey during our lifetime? Do we believe we are being transformed, from one degree of glory to the next? It's our confession of faith that often carries us through. Are we agreeing with what God promises in His Word, or are we allowing our mouths to agree more with the enemy of our souls? <u>Our journey is a heart process</u>.

Years ago there was a faith movement where believers would claim a Bible verse and believe God would do it. There was some truth in this, but many immature people used it more as a "name it and claim it" game, and they were often disappointed. <u>There is a fine line between presumption and faith</u>; but as we mature, we come to understand how to use God's Word.

As we progress on our journey of faith, <u>the journey that takes us to the high places of the presence of the Lord</u>, the question remains: <u>What do we say along the way, to ourselves and to others?</u> If the Word is not hidden in our hearts, we may murmur and complain. We may speak about all our doubts and fears. But God wants us to declare His truth instead. *"Your word have I laid up in my heart, that I might not sin against You." Psalm 119:11*

How can we journey on, especially in times of darkness, without a light to show us the way? *Psalm 119:105 "Your word is a lamp to my feet and a light to my path."* The challenge is to keep aligning our hearts, our minds, and our words with God's truth. *Isaiah 55:11 "So shall My word be that goes forth out of My mouth; it shall not return to Me void (without producing any effect, useless), but it shall accomplish that which I please and purpose, and it shall prosper in the thing for which I sent it."* Sound always precedes manifestation, so our voices need to declare truth, and thanksgiving always precedes miracles. So let us see it, speak it, then give thanks.

Our words matter when we pray and intercede and when we testify to others. *Hebrews 10:23 : "So let us seize and hold fast and retain without wavering the hope we cherish and confess and our acknowledgement of it, for He Who promised is reliable (sure) and faithful to His word."*

Our confession of faith is powerful. When declaring God's truth becomes a habit in our daily lives, we will be better prepared for times of crisis. Over the years as I've prayed and interceded for all my beloved family members, I've been encouraged with these words that have become my personal confession of faith. It's a truth I know with all my heart: *"For I know in whom I have believed and am persuaded (convinced) that He is able to guard and keep all that has been entrusted to me, and which I've committed to Him, until that day." (II Timothy 1:12)*

6. Write out your confession of faith here.

_____

_____

_____

Journeying to the High Places...

When I first became a Christian, I discovered the beautiful and profound allegory called *Hind's Feet on High Places* by Hannah Hurnard (which I mentioned earlier). I saw my own journey as I read the pages, and I found myself re-reading the book every ten years, seeing new depth each year. The book is about the journey we all take to know the Kingdom of God's love and to be able to leap from each challenge to the next as a dear or mountain goat might do.

Habakkuk 3:18-19 "Yet I will rejoice in the Lord; I will exult in the (victorious) God of my salvation! The Lord God is my Strength, my personal bravery, and my invincible army; He makes my feet like hinds' feet and will make me to walk (not to stand still in terror, but to walk) and make (spiritual) progress upon my high places (of trouble, suffering, or responsibility)!"

The book's journey starts with the seed of God's love planted in the heart of little Much-afraid, and she ventures on with her Good Shepherd always near. Although she goes through challenging times and finds herself in difficult places, her Guide brings her through to reach the high places of His Kingdom. There God's promises to her come to pass; she is completely healed, transformed, and given a new name. This is not when she gets to heaven, but rather when she begins to live the abundant life Jesus talked about in *John 10*. She begins to see her destiny fulfilled. Along the way, she doesn't know how she will get there, but she learns clearly that He is with her on her journey and that He is faithful to help her. God is promising to do the same for all of us.

"And I will bring the blind by a way that they know not: I will lead them in paths that they have not known. I will make darkness into light before them and make uneven places into a plain. These things I have determined to do (for them); and I will not leave them forsaken." Isaiah 42:16 And David also spoke of this journey when he wrote in *Psalm 18:33, "He makes my feet like hinds' feet (able to stand firmly or make progress on the dangerous heights of testing and trouble); He sets me securely upon my high places."*

7. What obstacles have you faced or might you face on your journey?

_____

_____

8. Describe what security in the high places would mean to you.

_____

_____

_____

Enduring with joy...

There was a time when I was facing a trial very similar to one I had recently gone through. The thought filled me with dread. "How can I go through that again, Lord?" I prayed. But I felt strongly that there was no way out but to go through it. So I prayed, "Lord, I'm willing to go through this again, but this time I would ask that You help me endure these circumstances with joy."

And God, in His loving kindness and great faithfulness, heard my prayer. I went through the trial for several years, but they were some of the sweetest years of my Christian life. The situation did not improve, but God went deep into my heart during those years, to uproot longings that were binding me and to set me free. I call those years my "Roter Rooter" years, and I wouldn't trade them for anything. May you too learn that enduring with joy is for you.

"Now may the God Who gives the <u>power of patient endurance (steadfastness), and Who supplies encouragement</u>, grant you to live in such mutual harmony and such full sympathy with one another, in accord with Christ Jesus, that together you may (unanimously) with united hearts and one voice, praise and glorify the God and Father of our Lord Jesus Christ (the Messiah)." Romans 15:5-6

More than conquerors...

Perhaps the most important advice to give anyone who is going through challenging moments in their faith journey is this: **Never give up.** A favorite truth of mine in the Bible is *"And it came to pass..."* <u>Every trial has an end, and God's will is that it brings us into victory.</u>

Perhaps the chapter that has meant the most to me in my journey of faith is **Romans 8**, the whole chapter. **<u>Verse 29</u>** tells us God has destined us to be molded into the image of His Son, and **<u>verse 30</u>** explains how He has called, justified, made righteous, and even glorified us. Then **verses 31 -32** *"What then shall we say to (all) this: <u>If God is for us, who (can be) against us,</u> (Who can be our foe, if God is on our side?) He who did not withhold or spare (even) His own Son but gave Him up for us all, <u>will He not also with Him freely and graciously give us all (other) things</u>?"*

Let us never forget that Jesus Himself is walking with us as we journey on and as we intercede for others **(verse 34).** Then the chapter concludes with **verses 35-39:** *"<u>Who shall ever separate us from Christ's love</u>? Shall suffering and affliction and tribulation? Or calamity and distress? Or persecution or hunger or destitution or peril or sword? Even as it is written, For Thy sake we are put to death all the day long; we are regarded and counted as sheep for the slaughter. Yet amid all these things <u>we are more than conquerors</u> and gain a <u>surpassing victory</u> through Him Who loved us. For I am persuaded beyond doubt (am sure) that neither death nor life, nor angels nor principalities, nor things impending and threatening nor things to come, nor powers, nor height nor depth, <u>nor anything else in all creation will be able to separate us from the love of God which is in Christ Jesus our Lord</u>."*

9. What is your favorite part of these verses in **Romans 8**?

_____

_____

_____

II Corinthians 2:14 "But thanks be to God, Who in Christ always <u>leads us in triumph (as trophies of Christ's victory)</u> and through us spreads and makes evident the fragrance of the knowledge of God everywhere." Never forget God is there to lead and guide us into victory.

Establishing a legacy of faith...

Hebrews 11 details a list of heroes of faith. ***Verse 2 "For by faith (trust and holy fervor born of faith) the men of old had divine testimony borne to them and obtained a good report."***

They lived their lives believing the promises of God, even if these promises were not fulfilled while they were on earth. ***Verse 13 "These people all died controlled and sustained by their faith, but not having received the tangible fulfillment of (God's) promises, only having seen it and greeted it from a great distance by faith, and all the while acknowledging and confessing that they were strangers and temporary residents and exiles upon the earth."***

This reminds me that the journey of faith is more about the *process* than the *outcome*. We don't walk in faith in order to get our way, but rather because it *is* the way of life, the way to know God. ***John 14:6 "Jesus said to him, I am the Way and the Truth and the Life; no one comes to the Father except by (through) Me."***

When we live a life of faith, we leave a powerful legacy to those who come after us. When we have a heritage of faith to remember, we are blessed. Not everyone has ancestors and even parents they are proud of. I know many people grow up in dysfunctional families, and my heart (and the Father's) breaks at the suffering some go through. The challenges some people face because of their upbringing may be tremendous, but overcoming dysfunction, even an abusive or horrible heritage, is possible with Jesus, our Redeemer. Generational curses can be broken and negative patterns can all be transformed by the power of the Gospel. When you are saved, you may be establishing a new lineage for your family.

I often reflect on my parents and ancestors. What a priceless gift to have a godly heritage. Remember the old hymn: *Faith of our Fathers?* The chorus says *"Faith of our fathers, holy faith. We will be true to Thee till death."*

My mother once told me that my Grandmother, Marie, in Norway (whom I never met and heard little about) had a favorite life verse. This verse has also come to be an encouraging life verse for me and one I've passed on to my daughter and grandchildren. ***Isaiah 41:10 "Fear not (there is nothing to fear), for I am with you; do not look around you in terror and be dismayed, for I am your God. I will strengthen and harden you to difficulties, yes, I will help you; yes, I will hold you up and retain you with My (victorious) right hand of rightness and justice."***

Steve Green sings a powerful song, *Find us Faithful*. It begins with the picture of our godly ancestors lining the way of our paths, cheering and encouraging us on in our journey of faith. Then he sings "Let us run the race not only for the prize, but may all who come behind us find us faithful. May the fire of our devotion light their way. May the footprints that we leave, lead them to believe and the lives we live inspire them to obey. Oh, may all who come behind us find us faithful."

If we have a God-fearing, loving heritage that has been passed on to us, we should thank our dear Lord for it every day. If not, we are able to start that godly lineage with our lives of faith.

10. Describe your heritage. Did your ancestors know the Lord? Did they have a life verse that you still remember?

_____

_____

_____

_____

11. What spiritual riches would you like to leave behind for your children and grandchildren?

_____

_____

_____

_____

Chapter 11:
The Concerns of the Creator

"Looking at Creative Intercession"

Intercession is making a connection...

As I have been writing this study, I have tried to express that intercession isn't always a dedicated time of prayer, but rather a life-style. I have been impressed with how God has been faithful to weave together many prayers and events of my life over the years to create an intercessory tapestry that would bring Him glory. ***"But (the time is coming when) the earth shall be <u>filled with the knowledge of the glory of the Lord</u> as the waters cover the sea." Habakkuk 2:14***

I'm praying that God would open our eyes to see more of what creative intercession is and that we will be encouraged to recognize this as a more vital part of our daily lives. <u>May God continue to reveal the different ways we are actually interceding</u> for people, for our country, and for the world we inhabit.

My hope in this chapter is to emphasize the depth and breadth of creative intercession and to help you explore how it connects to the heart of the Creator God.

For many years I have thanked God for the precious intercessors I have known and learned from. Surely <u>God's mercy and grace are clearly evident in our cities and nations because of the many dedicated saints who have connected to the heart of God</u>. They have reached up to heaven and brought God's Kingdom into many situations. They have *connected their lives to the Creator of heaven and Earth.* It is this last phrase best that best expresses what I am learning about effective and creative intercession. Intercession means connection. However, intercession is not just connecting with people or situations in need, for that could overwhelm us if we remained there. It is rather <u>connecting with them *for the purpose of bringing them to the power of the Gospel...connecting them to their Redeemer.*</u>

Our words and deeds, in fact our very presence, are the means by which some are connected to the heart of God. <u>When we live filled with the Holy Spirit, His life is released to touch others</u>. As His vessels for peace, it's up to us to keep our hearts pure enough to let the love of God flow through us. If our hearts are filled with earthly things, like our cares, our doubts, or our fears, we may be blocking that flow. <u>May our prayers be filled instead with hope and faith based on God's truth so that His Spirit may be released into the atmosphere around us.</u> ***Ephesians 3:10 "(The purpose is) that through the church the complicated many-sided <u>wisdom of God in all its infinite variety and innumerable aspects might now be made known to the angelic rulers and authorities (principalities) and powers) in the heavenly sphere.</u>"***

We may never be able to share the Gospel with certain people, and we may never see salvation or a breakthrough in a certain situation; but <u>while we are on earth, we can lift all that concerns us before God in prayer and leave the results to Him.</u> One day in heaven we may stand amazed at what our simple lives of intercession actually accomplished. Someone we may even have forgotten may approach us to say, "Thank you. It was your life of prayer that brought me here." What a wonderful privilege we have to connect individuals to their Creator. As we pray, <u>may we ask our Creator Father what is on His heart for each of them</u> for He loves them more than we do.

1. What have you done or do you want to do to connect someone to their Redeemer in prayer?

_____

_____

_____

Imagination leads to creation...

<u>The realm of faith is a realm of imagination or vision, and it is essential to our Christian health.</u> ***"Where there is no vision (no redemptive revelation of God), the people perish;" Proverbs 29:18a.*** My vision or hope is to see God's Kingdom established on Earth through our faith-filled prayers, and I believe it is <u>our creative intercession</u> that He uses to do this.

<u>To create means "to make</u> (or cause to be) <u>or to become</u> (or to bring into existence)." That's what God did when He created the vast heavens, the whole earth, and mankind in its diversity. As we look at the book of ***Genesis***, we see the role of each member of the Trinity: Father, Spirit, and Son. ***John 1:1*** explains how <u>Jesus was there at the time of creation with the Father</u>. ***"In the beginning (before all time) was the Word (Christ), and the Word was with God, and the Word was God Himself."*** ***Genesis 1:2-3*** says ***"<u>The Spirit of God was moving</u> (hovering, brooding) over the face of the waters. And God said, Let there be light; and there was light."*** So when we think of creation, we are referring to the work of Father, Son, and Holy Spirit.

Genesis 1:26 "God said, Let us (<u>Father, Son, and Holy Spirit) make mankind in Our image</u>, after Our likeness, and let them have complete authority..." So if God is our Creator and we are in His image, <u>doesn't He expect us also to create</u>? This is explained in ***Colossians 2:9-10. "For in Him the***

whole fullness of Deity (the Godhead) continues to dwell in bodily form (giving complete expression of the divine nature). And <u>you are in Him, made full and having come to fullness of life (in Christ you too are filled with the God-head—Father, Son and Holy Spirit</u>—and reach full spiritual stature). And <u>He is the Head of all rule and authority</u> (of every angelic principality and power)."

If you've never felt you were very creative, why not ask God now to reveal the creativity that is within you. We are equipped, as God's creation, <u>to imagine new things</u> and to envision new realities for ourselves and others. And we have <u>God's authority to speak these things into existence</u>. That's what creative intercession means. <u>Intercession means to connect others to God, and *creative intercession takes it to the point of making God's will a reality*</u>.

Father God first imagined or envisioned what He wanted to create, next it was spoken, and then it was created. <u>Doesn't that describe a life of faith and what we do as intercessors</u>? First we are to <u>envision</u> God's purposes according to His Word; then we are to <u>believe</u> His promises and <u>speak</u> them into the atmosphere. In that sense, <u>all we pray for in faith is an act of creating a new reality. Envisioning, believing, and speaking truth are the essence of a life of faith</u>.

2. What have you imagined for a loved one, and what promise has God given you in His Word?

_____

_____

_____

The midnight hour...

"Weeping may endure for a night, but joy comes in the morning." Psalm 30:5 That's always hopeful news, but when does the morning come? It's good to notice that <u>a day with God doesn't actually begin when the sun comes up, but rather the evening before</u>. *Genesis 1:13 "And there was evening and there was morning, a third day."* Why is that important? Because as we intercede, God hears our prayers and answers, but it may be the midnight hour, with several more hours needed before a new day begins. We are never to doubt in the darkness what God has shown us in the light. When darkness and delay come, <u>God wants us to trust Him that a new day will eventually come</u>...joy indeed will come in the morning.

After all the dark days of testing that Job endured, he said in *Job 19:25 "For I know that my Redeemer and Vindicator lives, and <u>at last He (the Last One) will stand upon the earth</u>."* Remember how the angel told Daniel *"Fear not, Daniel, for <u>from the first day that you set your mind and heart to understand and to humble yourself before your God, your words were heard</u>." (* See *Daniel 10:12-13)* Even though there was a delay in God's response, God proved His faithfulness. And let us not forget that when Jesus' friend Lazarus died, Jesus waited four days before he performed the resurrection miracle. He said to his sister, ***"Did I not tell you and promise you that <u>if you would believe and rely on Me, you would see the glory of God</u>?" John 11:40*** Let us remember that when we are in dark times, <u>we are not in the tomb but in the womb</u> (as Joel Osteen once said). <u>New life will come in the morning, so hold on and trust in God's goodness.</u>

3. What hour do you think you might be in with your prayer and how is your faith doing?

_____

_____

_____

To dream the impossible dream…

One of my favorite songs was "The Quest" from the musical ***Man of La Mancha***. If you are familiar with the idealist Don Quixote, you may recognize that he was a symbol of seeing the good in people and situations and believing in the redemption of all things, even the worst impossibilities. The musical captured his spirit with words like *"to dream the impossible dream, to fight the unbeatable foe, to bear with unbearable sorrow, to go where the brave dare not go… This is my quest, to follow that star, no matter how hopeless, no matter how far…to reach the unreachable star."* <u>That always reminded me of the calling of faith, knowing all things are possible with God</u>. ***"But Jesus looked at them and said, With men this is impossible, but all things are possible with God." Matthew 19:26***

Has God given you a dream for something? Think of all that has been created because of a dream or vision. Angels and animals don't have dreams, but people are by nature dreamers. <u>We hold dreams in our hearts, even though we don't always see them become realities</u>. It <u>often takes risk and investment and time</u>, lots of time. Think of the spiritual implications here. Are we willing to invest time and prayer to see God's promise become a reality? Often our fears, doubts, and discouragement shut down our dreams and weaken our faith; but as we persevere and refuse to give up, God's will shall be done. <u>God puts the power of creation in a dream</u>, in our imagination. <u>God refines our dream as we lean on Him</u>, and <u>He may unlock</u> <u>our destiny or the destiny of others through our dreams and our creative intercession.</u>

As we intercede, <u>we see the need and connect it to God's Word of hope</u>. Then we <u>imagine and dream</u> (in faith), <u>making petition with</u> <u>thanksgiving and rejoicing</u>. We declare the Word and <u>hold fast our confession of faith</u>. ***"You will make your prayer to Him, and He will hear you… <u>You shall also decide and decree a thing, and it shall be established for you</u>; and the light (of God's favor) shall shine upon your ways…<u>He will even deliver the one (for whom you intercede) who is not innocent</u>; yes, he will be delivered through the cleanness of your hands."*** (See ***Job 22:27-30***.)

144

4. What is or was your dream for yourself or someone else?

    _____

    _____

    What "investment" may be needed to see it come to pass?

    _____

    _____

    _____

    _____

His creative Word and intercession...

It's not a surprise that God's Word has great power in intercession. After all, in the beginning was the Word and He created all heaven and earth. Is anything too difficult for the Master Creator? Our challenges are quite small compared to the immensity of creating the entire universe. May God change our perspective to see things more as He does and to recognize the power at work through His Gospel.

The Word of God, as it is confessed by believers, is a powerful intercessory weapon to tear down strongholds, to release captives, to bring forth blessing, and to establish God's Kingdom purposes on this Earth. How could we think of going into a battle with our sword still in its sheath, or even worse, left behind on our night stand at home?

A dear pastor of mine, now with the Lord, used to remind us of how Jesus Himself defeated the enemy by responding to him with, "It is written..." and then declaring God's truth. This is a powerful tool that transforms the darkest atmosphere. Never forget this truth: ***"So shall My word be that goes forth out of My mouth: it shall not return to Me void (without producing any effect, useless), but it shall accomplish that which I please and purpose, and it shall prosper in the thing for which I sent it." Isaiah 55:11*** May we be God's mouthpiece in our intercession.

Many books also have explored the power of confessing God's Word. In this brief study, I am only attempting to approach this subject. I would like, however, to remind us again of a verse to hold onto when life seems to put you up against the enemy of your soul:

"And they have overcome (conquered) him by means of the blood of the Lamb and by the utterance of their testimony, for they did not love and cling to life even when faced with death (holding their lives cheap till they had to die for their witnessing)." Revelation 12:11

This verse sums up how our words, connected with the Gospel, bring us victory over our enemy. We are indeed more than conquerors when our heart believes and trusts in the power of Christ's shed blood and our lives bear witness to that truth. But we need to confess that which is true and possible with God instead of the negative aspects seen in the "natural." This passage concludes with the reminder that some victories are only seen with our sincere attitude of surrender. God is looking for the same overcoming attitude in us that Jesus expressed in Gethsemene when He concluded, *"Nevertheless, not my will but Thine be done."*

This humble attitude of surrender to the sovereignty of the Lord is far from the presumptuous "name it and claim it" practice that has trapped some Christians in recent years. It is not enough just to confess God's truth. God always looks at our hearts. I appreciated Chuck Pierce's definition in *The Worship Warrior:* "*Presumption is speaking beyond your level of faith, beyond the bounds of your faith.*" A deep surrender to the Wisdom of God is never a compromise of our faith. On the contrary, surrendering our own will to the will of God is absolute faith, the purest faith. This faith is not in what God can and might do, not even in what He says, but rather in *who He is.* And that's the faith that can move mountains.

The most effective warrior in God's army carries his sword (the Word of God) faithfully, holding it close to their heart at all times, wielding it as the Spirit leads. For in every instance of intercession this is true: *It is "'not by might, nor by strength, but by My Spirit,' says the Lord of Hosts. 'This mountain shall be removed, by my Spirit,' says the Lord." (Zechariah 4:6).* It is Christ alone who has overcome the world; our confession simply connects us to that reality.

And, once again, when we are at a loss as to what words to even say or pray, we can rely on the Holy Spirit in us. Let us remember this promise in *Romans 8:26-27: "So too the Holy Spirit comes to our aid and bears us up in our weakness; for we do not know what prayer to offer nor how to offer it worthily as we ought, but the Spirit Himself goes to meet our supplication and pleads in our behalf with unspeakable yearning and groanings too deep for utterance, and He who searches the hearts of men knows what is in the mind of the Holy Spirit (what His intent is) because the Spirit intercedes and pleads (before God) in behalf of the saints according to and in harmony with God's will."*

5. Think back on when you have confessed His Word concerning a person or situation and felt the power of the Spirit rise up in you so strong that you knew your words broke through something in the heavenlies. Could you describe this time here?

_____

_____

_____

_____

The power of Worship Intercession...

Intercession takes many forms, but I believe all Christians have experienced some times of worship intercession. There are two great books that deal with intercession and worship: *The Worship Warrior* and *Worship as it is in Heaven,* both by Chuck Pierce and John Dickson, his worship leader. These books do an excellent job on the subject, so my efforts here are mainly to encourage you to look at these books if worship and intercession both stir your heart. On page 193 of *The Worship Warrior*, Chuck writes: *"When we worship and intercede, we tear down the snares that have been erected in the earth by our enemy. God has a process of manifesting His will on earth. Worship invades each one of the steps of that process."* Then he goes on to explain the process, but again I encourage you to read these pages for yourself.

I'd like to emphasize worship again because God has shown me how often my songs and worship to Him have been a type of intercession or a point of connection. Have you ever felt God's powerful presence when you were singing in a church service? Has a new song to the Lord ever come into your heart? I know some of my best times of worship and intercession were when I was alone in my car during a long commute to work. I was once told that in a dark or <u>desperate time, it is most helpful to play Christian worship music 24/7</u> in your home to establish a protective covering.

Often the <u>lyrics of our hymns and choruses are deep prayers of intercession</u>. Lately I've been impressed, as I listen to certain worship CD's, that I am hearing vocalists intercede. The lyrics connect me to my Lord, and I've felt His grace released just by listening. For example, consider how these words are often sung in intercession for our nation: *"God bless America, land that I love. Stand beside her and guide her through the night with a light from above."* Perhaps there has never been a time in our history when these words were needed more, for truly only God can guide and heal our land.

Moreover, I've been especially blessed in recent years to have the Holy Spirit give me a song from "out of nowhere" that would speak to a situation I was praying about. I love it when I receive a song because I know it's not just my thoughts that could have brought this forth. Most of these songs are hymns from my distant past, and I don't even know the words until I look them up and see what God has to say. It's a wonderful gift from the Holy Spirit and has encouraged me through some very dark times. God knows the prayers on my heart, and <u>when I connect with His heart through praise and worship, His power is released</u> to transform the natural. Let me share an example with you.

You may know that my dear brother was brutally murdered a few years ago. This tragedy has brought me much closer to looking at life through God's lens of eternity. I know this excruciating loss has been redeemed, and that one day we will see it all more clearly. But for now, I've learned to let go, forgiving the wretched and blind perpetrators of such a cruel crime, and trusting God to bring my family peace.

At times, however, I struggled with what happened and have asked God, "If I'm an intercessor, why didn't You put it on my heart to be praying especially hard for my brother prior to his death? We should have known to help him with the situation he was in. Perhaps it's my lack of intercession that permitted his abuse and the ultimate cruelty to take place."

However, by God's grace I did not linger in that negative guilt trap. I've learned over the years not to dwell on such thoughts, knowing that any self-accusation comes from the accuser of the brethren himself. I know *there is absolutely no condemnation in Jesus Christ (*see *Romans 8:1, 33-34)*. Nevertheless, I couldn't let go of the nagging regret that I didn't intercede enough, both physically and spiritually, for my brother...until...

One day the Holy Spirit reminded me of what I had been doing just three weeks prior to my brother's murder. I had driven alone to Lake Chelan to spend the weekend with my daughter's family at our timeshare condo. Interestingly enough, I was looking forward to the 3 ½ hour drive over and back. I brought along a supply of worship CD's and played them continually both ways. I sang my heart out to God. It was one of the most refreshing and energizing times of worship I've ever known—just me, the recording saints, and God.

What really was happening during those 7 hours of worship? Someday I will know, but for now I believe that those seven hours released great spiritual power, perhaps even angels, into the earthly realm. God's Spirit was being unleashed to move into all the areas that I was committing to Him. I may not have known at the time what my brother was facing or what he was about to go through, but GOD DID. God would sustain and cushion my brother with His grace, and His angels would minister to him before they ushered him home to the very throne room of God. I know my brother did not face his enemies alone any more than our Lord did when he was crucified. What appeared to be a horrible win for the enemy may actually have been a moment of victory for my brother, even as the cross was for Jesus.

After his death, I saw in my spirit a comforting image. I saw a standing ovation in heaven when my brother entered after having completed his earthly journey. Things on earth are not all that God sees from His perspective; we need eternal eyes to see beyond the natural. Our thoughts just are not yet high enough to be God's thoughts on such things, but He's giving us hints that there's so much more going on than we can fathom while in this earthly realm. I praise the Lord for that great consolation. And so I was encouraged that I had done my part just by worshipping the only One who could truly intercede for my brother.

6. Can you share a time when praise and worship was clearly a time of intercession?

_____

_____

Artistic intercession...

When I first thought of this study, I wanted to explore the many diverse and creative ways God has led us to intercede. So let's reflect on and share some of these most meaningful times...remembering that <u>our prayers are connected to the Creator of all things, so some intercession may be very different and creative</u>.

Let's think about the arts a minute. In addition to <u>singing, there's drawing, painting, sculpting, dancing, instrument playing, poetry, storytelling, photography, culinary arts, gardening, etc. The list seems endless</u>. Could any facet of art actually be an expression of intercession, a means of connecting the natural to the divine? After all, ***"The earth is the Lord's, and the fullness of it, the world and they who dwell in it." Psalm 24:1*** God seems to be opening my eyes to see how vast intercession really is and how I truly am interceding even at times when I am not in a physical posture of prayer.

For example, creating a painting can be an act of intercession. <u>God puts an impression on an artist's heart and as he or she puts it on canvas, it becomes an expression of the heart of God</u> concerning a certain matter. The artist may have no idea where the painting will lead, but as he or she begins to apply paint to a canvas, the Holy Spirit directs until it reveals what God intended. As we paint or as we behold what was created, <u>we find ourselves interceding</u> for that matter, and a divine connection has been made. Prophetic art is being seen more and more in the body of Christ. Some churches have prophetic artists who paint as the Spirit leads while someone is preaching. People who may not even know they had a talent for drawing, painting, or sculpting are being <u>led to express the heart of God through beautiful and provocative works of art.</u>

Other ordinary objects can also be instruments of intercession. Almost every painting or plaque in my home represents something the Lord is saying to me, has done in my life, or something I'm hoping to see manifested. <u>Some of us are just drawn to look at the natural and see the spiritual or to see the symbolic meaning behind the ordinary things of life</u>. I know that is annoying to some people and makes us slightly "peculiar," but I believe that is because He has called me to be a creative intercessor who easily makes such connections. What I mean here is that <u>an object may be used to connect a person or a situation to God's throne</u> of intercession. For example, while I was doing office work for several years, I began to long to return to my teaching career. I had a small decorative student desk that I placed on my dresser as a <u>symbol of that "calling" and every time I looked at it, I thought about teaching</u>. Even if I wasn't praying audibly, I was interceding for myself in that role and for the children whose lives I would touch as a teacher. Then a few years later, God opened the way for me to once again teach children.

7. What role does any of the arts play in your life, and how might it be expressing what's on the Father's heart?

_____

_____

_____

_____

Acts of kindness...

If creative intercession means connecting things in the natural to God, think of all the <u>different ways we may be able to express God's heart to others</u>.

How could making and sending a card be an act of intercession? What about simple phone calls or text messages? Even a smile may send hope to another person.

My mother used to sew beautiful bridal gowns for her family and friends; what a wonderful expression of intercession that might have been. How about making a meal for someone or even cleaning a house? What about those who do physical jobs, like construction? <u>Could indeed all acts of kindness and creativity become acts of intercession</u>? Could doing an unexpected act of kindness be a more powerful spiritual act than ever imagined?

8. Thinking of all the expressions of the arts or crafts, what creative talents has God given you? If you don't feel very creative, what other things might you do to bless others?

_____

_____

_____

_____

9. Explain how God has used or could use random acts of kindness to fulfill His will.

_____

_____

_____

_____

God's acts and ways...

Perhaps intercessors are the most peculiar of God's chosen people. Indeed everyone in the body of Christ is part of a peculiar race, set apart to bring the glory of God into different circumstances. But sometimes intercessors notice and do more peculiar things than others do. Sometimes God will impress on an intercessor something he/she could do that makes no sense at the time. Sometimes it's a symbolic act or something in the natural that represents something in the spiritual. And if we ask God to reveal the meaning of such acts, He usually does in His perfect timing.

We recognize that God's thoughts are so much greater than ours, and His ways so far above our ways. That reminds me of Moses and the people of Israel. God called the Israelites to do certain things; He revealed His acts to them. They beheld the parting of the Red Sea and the water coming forth from a rock, all the result of *acts* performed by Moses. But God saw Moses as an intercessor for this people, so He revealed to him His *ways*, not just His acts. ***Psalm 103:7-8 "He made known His ways (of righteousness and justice) to Moses, His acts to the children of Israel. The Lord is merciful and gracious, slow to anger and plenteous in mercy and loving-kindness."*** That is the way of our Lord, to show mercy, love, and grace.

Sometimes we obediently act as God leads us without understanding why, but sometimes God reveals His ways (or His purposes) behind actions and happenings to His intercessors. Sometimes we just follow the cloud by day and the pillar of fire at night, trusting God has a way out of a difficult situation. Often it's not until the battle is over that we see how God's ways were there to bring us through. When at times we get hints of what God is doing behind the scenes, we are beginning to understand His ways.

10. Have you ever done something, either planned or done spontaneously, and later wondered why? What significance did that act have?

_____

_____

_____

_____

Working all out for good...

One "way" of God that I've noticed over the years is that God uses everything and wastes nothing; He is very economical. There are no mistakes with God. And if we make mistakes, God turns them around to create something good. But this happens best when we are God-dependent rather than self-dependent. When we depend fully on God, He takes the responsibility of caring for all our needs very seriously. After all, God knows how to take care of what belongs to him. ***"All things work together for good for those who are the called according to His purpose," Romans 8:28*** has been my life verse.

When I was going through my "Tunnel Years," I leaned on God's grace and depended on Him to provide a home for me and my family. It was a long, difficult journey that stretched my intercessory muscles beyond what I ever thought I could endure. This wilderness season seemed to be wrought with mistakes and challenges, on a very deep level. It was a profound lesson of trust, as we experienced the love of God firsthand. Through this time, I came to understand some differences between believing, having faith, and trusting. It seems to be that God's presence goes deeper and deeper into our souls as we lean on Him.

It starts with believing. **Believing is an act of the mind—**God had to change all of our minds many, many times during this trial and to restore or renew our minds to the mind of Christ or we would've fainted and entered into great despair.

Then our belief grows into a strong faith. **Faith is an act of the will—**As I've explained, God wants us not just to believe, but to have faith in Him by surrendering completely, utterly, to His sovereign will, to His goodness and love. The night I did that with our home was a turning point in this trial for me. I got up from my knees knowing, after three years, that whatever would happen, I knew it'd be okay because God is not only sovereign but totally good.

Finally, it results in trust. **Trust is an act of the heart—**The heart is the deepest part of our being and when belief and faith have done their work, true trust is born. The journey can be long; we try to trust, we think we trust, until again we are disappointed. But one day, at the end of a certain trial, we know the work is complete. There is a deep, abiding trust in our inmost being that nothing can shake. This is where Job was when he declared, ***"Though He slay me, yet will I trust Him." Job 13:15***

During testing timers, we need to cling to this advice each day. ***"Trust in the Lord with all your heart and lean not on your own understanding. In all your ways acknowledge Him and He will direct your path." Proverbs 3:5-6*** Remember His thoughts and ways are usually much higher than we can imagine, but as we learn to know God's character, we can let go and rest in His embrace.

Although our trials can be very costly in the natural, they will always be worth it all. I see it now as a reminder to keep my hope in the Lord instead of in things. As Paul said in ***Philippians 3:7-8, "But whatever former things I had that might have been gains to me, I have come to consider as one combined loss for Christ's sake. Yes, furthermore, I count everything as loss compared to the possession of the priceless privilege (the overwhelming preciousness, the surpassing worth, and supreme advantage) of knowing Christ Jesus my Lord..."*** Let us strive to gain Paul's perspective of what's important in life.

Think back about some peculiar or unusual things you have done, even mistakes, that you now recognize may have been led or used by the Lord, that His glory would be revealed.

11. Have you ever seen God redeem a situation or a mistake? How did He do that?

_____

_____

_____

_____

_____

_____

Chapter 12:
The Father's Heart

"Interceding as He would"

Each person's unique life...

When you began this study with me, perhaps you never considered yourself to be an intercessor. Granted there are some with a special calling to enter into intercessory prayer in a more powerful way, but my hope has been that each of us will see that our entire Christian life is full of intercession. We all are <u>called to connect the people and situations of our lives to our Father God through our prayers</u>. Each person is unique in who they are, where they are placed, and who their lives touch.

Although our lives are all different, we share a common calling. As Christians we are all called to <u>know God</u>, through His Son Jesus Christ, better and better, more and more fully, and to be His vessel on the earth. We don't wait to have eternal life when we die; we are called to live in it right now, each day. Jesus explained, ***"And <u>this is eternal life: (it means)</u> <u>to know</u> (to perceive, recognize, become acquainted with, and understand) You, the only true and real God, and (likewise) to <u>know Him</u>, Jesus (as the) Christ (the Anointed One, the Messiah), Whom You have sent." John 17:3.***

My prayer for you is in ***Ephesians 3,*** but especially ***verse 19: "<u>(That you may really come) to know</u> <u>(practically, through experience for yourselves) the love of Christ</u>, which far surpasses mere knowledge (without experience); that you may be filled (through all your being) unto all the fullness of God (may have the richest measure of the divine Presence, and become a body wholly filled and flooded with God Himself)!"*** <u>To know the love of Christ like this takes time and often trials</u>, but that should be the goal we strive toward.

As Paul expressed in ***Philippians 3:6 "<u>(For my determined purpose is) that I may know Him</u> (that I may progressively become more deeply and intimately acquainted with Him, perceiving and recognizing and understanding the wonders of His Person more strongly and more clearly), and that I may in that same way come to <u>know the power outflowing from His resurrection</u> (which it exerts over believers)..."***

My hope in this final chapter is that you will see how you've grown closer to the heart of our Father God through His powerful Word and that you will be encouraged and victorious in your prayers of intercession.

As baby Christians we don't automatically know all about God; we grow in our understanding much as our children grow to know us throughout their lives. It takes time and life's hard times to learn to appreciate the fullness of God's character. That is, we may know in our heads that God is Love and that He's always faithfully with us, but it's not until we see that truth evidenced in our own experiences, that we really know it in our hearts. That's when our knowing becomes unshakeable.

That is why we are able to count it all joy when we go through life's challenges. God is using everything we go through to bring us closer to Him, to help us know Him better and better, and to transform us more into His likeness. *James 1:2-4 "**Consider it wholly joyful**, my brethren, whenever you are enveloped in or encounter trials of any sort or fall into various temptations. Be assured and understand that the trial and proving of your faith bring out endurance and steadfastness and patience, but let endurance and steadfastness and patience have full play and do a thorough work, so that you may be (people) perfectly and fully developed (with no defects), lacking in nothing."* Let us not forget that even Jesus grew in wisdom and stature and favor with God and men. *(Luke 2:52)*

*"Now may the **God of peace** (Who is the Author and the Giver of peace), Who brought again from among the dead our Lord Jesus, that great Shepherd of the sheep, by the blood (that sealed, ratified) the everlasting agreement (covenant, testament) strengthen (complete, perfect) and make you what you ought to be and equip you with everything good that you may carry out His will; (while He Himself) works in you and accomplishes that which is pleasing in His sight, through Jesus Christ (the Messiah); to Whom be the glory forever and ever (to the ages of the ages). Amen (so be it)." Hebrews 13:20-21* May we enjoy our journey of knowing and growing.

1. According to the verses above, explain in what ways you have grown in knowing God.

_____

_____

_____

_____

We start as babies and learn to sit...

When we reflect on our Christian life and growth, it's sometimes good to see how far we've come. Consider how a baby develops. First it can only lie down, but soon it learns to sit up. That is how we are to grow as Christians. As soon as we are born of His Spirit, we are seated with Christ. *"And **He raised us up together with Him and made us sit down together (giving us joint seating with Him) in the heavenly sphere** (by virtue of our being) in Christ Jesus (the Messiah, the Anointed One)."*

Ephesians 2:6 <u>Even though our bodies are still in this world, the truth is we are spiritually seated</u> <u>in the heavenlies, not to be limited by our earthly reality</u>. Unfortunately we aren't always taught this truth or we forget it as life goes on. We may get frustrated as <u>we try to stand up, walk, and even run</u> <u>before we learn to sit with Jesus.</u>

When a baby grows from lying down to sitting up, <u>it is a vital time for it to interact more fully</u> with the world around it, to discover itself, to respond to the voices it hears, and to learn to smile. <u>A baby</u> <u>can't stand, walk or run at first, but grows greatly during the important stage of sitting</u>. As new Christians, we should first come to understand that we are seated with Christ and all that means, even though we are still living on earth.

It is <u>when we are seated in Christ that we learn best</u> *Who He is and who we are*. ***"And (so that you*** ***can*** <u>**know and understand**</u> ***what is the immeasurable and unlimited and surpassing greatness*** ***of*** <u>**His power in and for us who believe**</u>***… Ephesians 1:19 "For*** <u>**we are God's (own) handiwork (His**</u> <u>**workmanship**</u>***), recreated in Christ Jesus, (born anew) that we may do those good works which*** ***God predestined (planned beforehand)… Ephesians 2:10*** Learning these truths while sitting with Him, <u>we grow to understand His powerful goodness and to accept ourselves, making peace with our</u> <u>weaknesses.</u> It is not a time to wallow in guilt or self-pity, but rather to get strengthened by repenting of sins and being nourished with His Truth.

<u>When we are seated in the heavenlies with Jesus, it is a position of authority and rest</u>. However, we must <u>choose to keep our heart, our spiritual life, there</u>. God gives us free will, and we choose how to view our lives and how to spend our time each day. <u>Just as Mary chose to sit at Jesus' feet</u> while Martha busied herself with other matters (see ***Luke 10:38-42***.), we also choose. Of course, we still live in this world and must do what's needed each day, but <u>we either do these things with our heart</u> <u>at rest (seated with Christ) or with our heart troubled by and responding to all the needs around us</u>. When we spend time sitting with Jesus, <u>we get prepared for what lies ahead of us</u>. Sitting is a position of rest, and we actually never grow out of our need to rest in Jesus.

<u>Truly everything we ever do as Christians should be done from a position of rest</u>. We are to learn to approach life with this attitude, <u>sitting down with Jesus on the inside, no matter what's happening</u> around us. Nevertheless, let us remember that we can't stay at rest when our souls are dealing with anger, fear, or worry. So before we lose our peace and get up and start running around in life, trying to fight our battles, <u>we need to sit at Jesus' feet and let Him show us how to resist such enemies</u> of our soul. ***"So be subject to God. Resist the devil (stand firm against him), and he will flee from*** ***you. Come close to God and He will come close to you." (James 4:7-8)***

<u>Rest is a position of power in the spiritual realm and perhaps our strongest weapon of warfare</u>. Just as we need physical rest to keep moving and be our best, we need spiritual rest to move forward in our Christian life. <u>Surely we don't expect a baby to stand, walk, or run before it learns to sit</u>. So why do we think we can move ahead without spending time with the Lord?

2. Have you ever felt the need to stop and rest in your spiritual journey? What can you learn as you sit at Jesus' feet and how does that <u>prepare you for standing strong, walking in faith, or running the race set before you</u>?

_____

_____

_____

_____

_____

The good, good Father...

Let's think a bit about the role of Father God. His essence gave us life. He knows us. ***Psalm 139*** is worth meditating on from time to time to remember that <u>we grow to know our Father because He already knows us</u>, even better than we know ourselves. In ***verse 1*** David reflects on how His Father has searched him: ***"O Lord, you have searched me (thoroughly) and <u>have known me</u>."*** But in ***verse 23*** he implores the Lord for more: ***"Search me (thoroughly), O God, and <u>know my heart</u>! Try me and know my thoughts! And see if there is any wicked or hurtful way in me, and lead me in the way everlasting."*** <u>David invites God into all the secret places of his heart so that there would be nothing hindering his closeness to his Father.</u>

<u>How well does Father God know each of us</u>? ***"<u>You know my downsitting and my uprising</u>; You <u>understand my thought</u> afar off. You sift and search out my path and my lying down, and You are <u>acquainted with all my ways</u>. For <u>there is not a word in my tongue (still unuttered), but, behold, O Lord, You know it altogether</u>. You have beset me and shut me in—behind and before, and You have laid Your hand upon me. Your (infinite) knowledge is too wonderful for me; it is high above me, I cannot reach it. Where could I go from Your Spirit? Or where could I flee from Your presence? Psalm 139:2-7*** These words should encourage us that <u>God knows everything we do and everywhere we go</u>. He knows all the cares of our hearts, what bothers us as well as what delights us. <u>He even knows our words before we say them</u>! That should give us great confidence as we pour out our hearts to Him.

While we are growing in the Lord, perhaps just learning to walk, we must always remember that we <u>have a loving Father helping us all the way</u>. <u>Father God will always pick us up when we fall</u> because He believes in us, strengthens us, and helps us walk because of His great love. ***"The steps*** *of a (good) man are directed and established by the Lord when He delights in his way (and He busies Himself with his every step), <u>though he falls, he shall not be utterly cast down, for the Lord grasps his hand in support and upholds him.</u>" Psalm 37:23-24*

Our loving Father knows us well, better than we know ourselves. <u>He knows our frame and all our frailties.</u> *"<u>As a father loves and pities his children, so the Lord loves and pities </u>those who fear Him (with reverence, worship, and awe), for <u>He knows our frame, He (earnestly) remembers and imprints (on His heart) that we are dust</u>." Psalm 103:13-14*

If I haven't convinced you yet about God's loving care for you, let me add these verses from ***Psalm 139:13-17*** *"For You did <u>form my inward parts;</u> You did knit me together in my mother's womb. I will confess and praise You for You are fearful and wonderful and for the awful wonder of my birth! Wonderful are Your works, and that my inner self knows right well. <u>My frame was not hidden</u> from You when I was being formed in secret and intricately and curiously wrought (as if embroidered with various colors) in the depths of the earth (a region of darkness and mystery). <u>Your eyes saw my unformed substance, and in Your book all the days of my life were written before ever they took shape,</u> when as yet there was none of them. <u>How precious and weighty also are Your thoughts to me, O God! How vast is the sum of them!</u>"* <u>If we meditate on these words even a bit, we will be convinced more than ever that God loves us and has a wonderful plan for our lives!</u>

3. Comment on how <u>understanding the love that Father God has for you</u> may help you in life. How well do you think He knows you?

_____

_____

_____

_____

_____

Growing in the Kingdom of God...

<u>Our unique journey is a *process* to establish our place in God's kingdom.</u> *Romans 14:17 "(After all) the <u>kingdom of God is not a matter of (getting the) food and drink</u> (one likes), but instead it is <u>righteousness</u> (that state which makes a person acceptable to God) and (heart) <u>peace and joy</u> in the Holy Spirit."* <u>Is this your goal in life?</u> Have you realized yet that earthly "success" is not enough?

I remember a time as a teenager (before I really began to walk with the Lord) when I first saw a verse on a church calendar that I took to heart. It said, ***"Blessed are those who hunger and thirst for righteousness for they shall be satisfied."*** As I read that verse, knowing little of the Bible, I said to God, "I do hunger and thirst for righteousness," and so God led me into His Kingdom. Here is that same verse as it is amplified in that translation: ***"Blessed and fortunate and happy and spiritually prosperous (in that state in which the born-again child of God enjoys His favor and salvation) are those who <u>hunger and thirst for righteousness</u> (uprightness and right standing with God), for they shall be completely satisfied!" (Matthew 5:6)***

<u>Just as we begin to know who we are in Christ by sitting with Him, we enter God's kingdom by first knowing our righteousness in Him.</u> ***Isaiah 64:6*** explains how our righteousness, (our best deeds of rightness and justice) is but filthy rags; we can never achieve right standing with God unless we see that <u>we are covered over by Jesus' robe of righteousness.</u> He paid the price for us that we could never pay to bring us into right standing with God. ***II Corinthians 5:21*** says ***"<u>For our sake He made Christ (virtually) to be sin Who knew no sin</u>, so that in and through Him we might become (endued with, viewed as being in, and examples of) <u>the righteousness of God</u> (what we ought to be, approved and acceptable and in right relationship with Him, by His goodness)."*** That is the unique truth of the Good News of God!

We begin our Christian journey by knowing it's not our goodness but Christ's sacrifice that brings us into right standing with God. So it is with our righteous living in the Kingdom of God. It's all because of Jesus. Many years ago, I felt the Lord impressing on my heart, "You will come to understand that the blood of Christ is enough." I think I'm finally catching on. Enough for what? Enough for everything. <u>The power truly is in the blood.</u> The power of the Gospel can and should be brought into all our circumstances. <u>That is how we live by faith and that is how we help bring His Kingdom to the Earth and into our lives. And that is our position in fruitful intercession.</u>

"For in the Gospel <u>a righteousness which God ascribes is revealed, both springing from faith and leading to faith</u> (disclosed through the way of faith that arouses to more faith). As it is written, The man who through faith is just and upright shall live and shall live by faith." Romans 1:17

God's Kingdom living leads us <u>from righteousness into peace and joy.</u> Once we understand our right-standing with God, <u>we enter into peace</u> (in our thoughts, words, and deeds) with our hearts in harmony with God's law of love. <u>From the place of peace, we begin to experience great joy</u>, no matter what happens in life. We learn to abide in His presence when we know this truth: ***"You will show me the path of life; <u>in Your presence is fullness of joy</u>, at Your right hand there are pleasures forevermore." Psalm 116:11*** And again in ***Acts 2:28 "You have made known to me the ways of life; <u>You will enrapture me (diffusing my soul with joy) with you and in Your presence.</u>"*** We begin to understand that the joy of the Lord is our strength. (See ***Nehemiah 8:10***.) As you search God's Word, may you see that God's truth was written to you ***"so that our joy (in seeing you included) may be full (and <u>your joy may be complete</u>). I John 1:4***

When our joy is complete is also when our trust in God is complete. As Christians we grow from believing God's promises (in our minds) to knowing them with all our hearts. That's how we become able to trust Him completely at all times, no matter what happens, but this growing process takes time. I hope we learn during this life process to enjoy the benefits of God's Kingdom: righteousness, peace, and joy.

4. How has the kingdom of God been made stronger, or more real, in your life?

_____

_____

_____

_____

Getting well dressed each day...

When you were a child, did you ever have the embarrassing dream of going to school in your pajamas? I remember many such dreams, and I find it curious that today's youth sometimes wear such clothes to school on purpose! Well, most of us, even today, still put some thought into what we are going to wear that would be suitable and comfortable for different occasions.

As we grow in our Christian life, we learn to stand our ground when things get hard. We stand on the promises we have received in the Word. The **sixth chapter of Ephesians (verses 13-18)** reminds us how to dress in the whole armor of God when we are in the position of standing. It reminds us to wear the belt of truth, the breastplate of integrity and righteousness, with our feet ready with the Gospel of peace, lifting up the shield of faith, and wearing the helmet of salvation. ***"Therefore put on God's complete armor, that you may be able to resist and stand your ground on the evil day (of danger), and having done all (the crisis demands), to stand (firmly in your place)." Ephesians 6:13*** Once we have spent time seated with Christ, knowing that He already won the war, we are able ***to "stand still and see the salvation of the Lord," (Exodus 14:13)*** for we know the battle belongs to the Lord. (See ***II Chronicles 20:15***.)

In addition to the armor listed in ***Ephesians 6***, we are told other things to put on each day. Great advice is given us in the ***third chapter of Colossians, Verses 12-13***, which tell us how to dress each day, by being humble, gentle, patient, and forgiving. Then ***Verse 14*** adds ***"And above all these (put on) love and enfold yourselves with the bond of perfectness (which binds everything together completely in ideal harmony)."*** Love is the appropriate clothing to wear each day as we relate to people, and we choose to wear it or not. ***John 13:35 "By this shall all (men) know that you are My disciples, if you love one another (if you keep on showing love among yourselves)."*** Remember the old chorus that says, "<u>They will know we are Christians by our love</u>?" Today such love is desperately needed; that is what the whole world is looking for.

If I were to add one more accessory to our essential Christian wardrobe, I would add the <u>right pair of glasses</u>. We need to look at life, at all that happens to us, to a loved one, or even to our nation, from God's perspective. <u>We need God's eternal perspective, eagle vision</u>, which we have from our place in the heavenlies, seated with Christ, and which enables us to see things more as He does.

5. Describe a situation you are facing now and describe how you need to "dress" for it.

_____

_____

_____

_____

_____

_____

Choosing what lens to look through...

One time in prayer I saw a picture of a box with a large banner covering it. I felt the Lord was saying that we too often put Him inside that box and let the cares of the world have freedom to cover our lives and the powerful goodness of God, like a heavy suffocating blanket. He said, "I would instead have you put all that concerns you in that box and <u>let the great rainbow of My covenant of love cover everything</u>." ***Colossians 3:23*** reminds us*: "And <u>**set your minds and keep them set on what is above**</u> **(the higher things), <u>not on the things that are on the earth</u>. For (as far as this world is concerned) you have died, and your (new, real) life is hidden with Christ in God."**

When my daughter was going through a long and difficult test, she asked me, "How do I know God doesn't want me to lose everything and to suffer more as the Apostle Paul did?" That was a good question. Why do some people go through unimaginable suffering? Only God knows the whole answer. I only know that <u>if we fear something, that fear never comes from the Father's heart of love</u>, and we need to resist it. Fear is always a dead-end road, but faith always leads us to a full future.

I also know that <u>His grace will always be sufficient for all we go through in life</u>. However, He never gives us that grace ahead of time, before it is needed. I often think of grace as being like the manna that God provided in the wilderness: <u>sufficient for each day, but not available until it is needed and not able to be stored for another day</u>. And I knew God will give her sufficient daily grace.

Then God reminded me that we need to see our lives through the <u>lens of His love</u>. Put on those glasses as you walk on in faith. That reminds me of a Righteous Brothers song I always loved: *"When you walk through a storm, hold your head up high, and don't be afraid of the dark. At the end of the storm, there's a golden sky, and the sweet silver song of a lark. Walk on through the wind, walk on through the rain, though your dreams be tossed and blown. Walk on, walk on, with hope in your heart, and you'll never walk alone. You'll never walk alone."* When life's darkness seems to surround you, <u>may God give you eyes to see the golden sky and ears to hear His voice</u>.

So what lens do you mostly look through? <u>We choose our focus or our lens each day</u>. Are we focused on the natural happenings around us, or <u>can we see life with eyes of hope and faith, trusting the goodness of God</u>? Are we near sighted or able to see from God's perspective, with the lens of eternity? Do we look at life through a lens of confidence and peace, or through a lens of doubt and fear? We choose each day how to see life.

Do you see all that happens in your life and in your intercessory prayers through the <u>lens of **"Christ, the Hope of (realizing the) glory**.</u>*"* *Colossians 1:27* Does that hope influence all you say and do each day? ***Colossians 3: 17*** adds *"And <u>**whatever you do (no matter what it is) in word or deed, do everything in the name of the Lord Jesus**</u> and in (dependence upon) His Person, giving praise to God the Father through Him."* Seeing life through that <u>leans of hope</u> gives us an attitude of gratitude.

And let us not forget the strength we have each day as we lean on the Lord. *"I have **<u>strength for all things in Christ</u>** Who empowers me (I am ready for anything and equal to anything through Him Who infuses inner strength into me; <u>I am self-sufficient in Christ's sufficiency</u>). Philippians 4:13*

6. Describe what lens you need to look through today and why?

_____

_____

_____

_____

_____

_____

_____

Enduring with joy and wisdom as we run our race...

Once we've begun to walk and even run in faith, there will be times when we are called to endure difficult things. Although we live in an "instant" world, this is not the way God produces lasting character in His people. A person's character is revealed and developed during the marathon of faith described in ***Hebrews 12:1 -2***. ***"Therefore then, since we are surrounded by so great a cloud of witnesses (who have borne testimony to the Truth), let us strip off and throw aside every encumbrance (unnecessary weight) and that sin which so readily (deftly and cleverly) clings to and entangles us, and let us run with patient endurance and steady and active persistence the appointed course of the race that is set before us, looking away (from all that will distract) to Jesus Who is the Leader and the Source of our faith (giving the first incentive for our belief) and is also its Finisher (bringing it to maturity and perfection)..."*** We are ***never*** in this marathon alone; we just need to look to Him for all we need. He will faithfully give us the grace to endure whatever comes our way.

Usually when we think we have to wait a long time for a breakthrough or to have patience in a difficult situation, we aren't too excited. Living in a "microwave" culture, we imagine (even dread) how hard it'll be to endure life's challenges. However, God would have us reach a place of maturity where we can endure whatever life brings us with a positive attitude of optimism and joy.

Remember how ***the first chapter of James*** tells us to count such times as joy? ***James 1:2 "Consider it wholly joyful, my brethren, whenever you are enveloped in or encounter trials of any sort or fall into various temptations."*** Once again, we are asked to consider it joyful; it's a choice we make. When we choose to see our trials more as God does, our faith is developing, as are our muscles of endurance, steadfastness, and patience. (See ***James 1:3-4***.) This is how we grow up or mature as Christians and how we develop Godly character.

Our joy and patience to endure trials depends on our perspective, but how are we able to see trials as God does? The first answer is God gives us grace for every situation that we face, grace to view life courageously. But to further help us, God gives us His perspective, His wisdom, which solidifies our faith. ***James 1:5-6*** encourages us: ***"If any of you is deficient in wisdom, let him ask of the giving God (Who gives) to everyone liberally and ungrudgingly, without reproaching or faultfinding, and it will be given him. Only it must be in faith that he asks with no wavering (no hesitating, no doubting). For the one who wavers (hesitates, doubts) is like the billowing surge out at sea that is blown hither and thither and tossed by the wind."***

To endure with joy, we need God's wisdom and His perspective. ***"But the wisdom from above is first of all pure (undefiled); then it is peace-loving, courteous (considerate, gentle). It is willing to yield to reason, full of compassion and good fruits; it is wholehearted and straight-forward, impartial and unfeigned (free from doubts, wavering, and insincerity)." James 3:17*** Let us never forget to ask for wisdom when we need it and then walk in it.

164

Our Christian life always leads us to times of endurance, but it has many rewards. Also in *James, chapter 1*, God explains why this happens. ***"Blessed (happy, to be envied) is the man who is <u>patient under trial and stands up under temptation, for when he has stood the test and been approved, he will receive (the victor's) crown of life,</u> which God has promised to those who love Him." James 1:12*** God is not trying to torture us with trials, but to crown us with blessing and victory.

7. Explain a time you've needed to endure and how God gave you wisdom to endure with joy.

_____

_____

_____

_____

_____

_____

The good fight of faith...

God sees everything from an eternal perspective. <u>He has our eternal heart in mind</u>, a heart that He hopes will reflect His own. ***"(You should) be exceedingly glad on this account, though now for a little while you may be distressed by trials and suffer temptations. <u>So that (the genuineness) of your faith may be tested, (your faith) which is infinitely more precious than the perishable gold</u> which is tested and purified by fire. (This <u>proving of your faith is intended) to redound when Jesus Christ (the Messiah, the Anointed One) is revealed</u>." I Peter 1:6-7***

As we learn to stand on God's Word and walk by faith, we all have our tough times. Our walk by faith is also a fight with the enemy of our souls. ***"<u>Fight the good fight of the faith;</u> lay hold of the eternal life to which you were summoned and (for which) <u>you confessed the good confession (of faith)</u> before many witnesses. " I Timothy 6:12***

Whether we think of enduring life's hard times as a marathon or a fight of faith, we keep pressing on until we get our second wind. Let us remember to <u>breathe in God's grace and breathe out our praise</u>. God is faithful to provide the grace to "press on" that we may endure with joy. And this grace or hope sometimes comes through other people. These verses have often brought me encouragement. ***"(What, what would have become of me) <u>had I not believed that I would see the Lord's goodness in the land of the living!</u> Wait and hope for and expect the Lord; be brave and of good courage and let your heart be stout and enduring. Yes, <u>wait for and hope for and expect the Lord</u>." Psalm 27:13-14***

As we go through life, we all need encouragement and hope. We need the strength of the Lord as well as His wisdom at all times, but especially during our trials. May we be certain to stir up this hope in ourselves and to spread it liberally to others. Let these words in **Romans 5** encourage you today: *"Through Him also we have (our) access (entrance, introduction) <u>by faith into this grace</u> (state of God's favor) in which we (firmly and safely) stand. And <u>let us rejoice and exult in our hope of experiencing and enjoying the glory of God.</u>*

"Moreover (let us also be full of joy now!) Let <u>us exult and triumph in our troubles and rejoice in our sufferings,</u> knowing that pressure and affliction and hardship produce patient and unswerving endurance.

"And <u>endurance (fortitude) develops maturity</u> of character (approved faith and tried integrity). And character (of this sort) produces (the <u>habit of joyful and confident hope</u> of eternal salvation.

"<u>Such hope never disappoints or deludes or shames us,</u> for God's love has been poured out in our hearts through the Holy Spirit Who has been given to us." Romans 5:2-5 (Sounds a lot like *James 1:2-4,* doesn't it?)

At the end of life, may we be able to declare: *"<u>I have fought the good (worthy, honorable, and noble) fight. I have finished the race. I have kept (firmly held) the faith</u>." II Timothy 4:7*

    8.   Reflect on the verses above and comment upon one part that gives you encouragement.

_____

_____

_____

_____

_____

_____

Courage, a heart connection...

As a language teacher, I notice that <u>the root of the word courage</u> was the same as the French word <u>"couer" which means "heart." So having courage is a heart issue.</u> I also think of en<u>courage</u>ment and dis<u>courage</u>ment and how they affect the heart. So it stands as a big warning that <u>we need to guard our heart and let God's words fill our heart daily.</u> *"For <u>they are life</u> to those who find them, <u>healing</u>*

***and health** to all their flesh. **Keep and guard your heart with all vigilance and above all that you guard**, for out of it flow the springs of life." Proverbs 4:22-23*

I remember when I was at a crisis times many years ago that Petra put out a song, "Don't let your heart get hardened." That was a warning to me that I paid attention to. When our heart is suffering, we are not able to live in the victory God would give us. Remember all the words of **Romans 8**? Paul shows us how to walk and pray in the Holy Spirit. He reminds us there is never condemnation for us because He is 100% for us. When He's on our side, who can stand against us? Paul also talks about the blessing of hope and how God will work out all things in our life. And the final verses are such a encouraging promise that absolutely nothing can ever separate us from Christ's love. Our knowing these truths deep in our heart causes us to become more than conquerors!

Another powerful reminder is **Joshua 1:9 *"Have I not commanded you? Be strong, vigorous, and very courageous. Be not afraid, neither be dismayed, for the Lord your God is with you wherever you go."*** I always think of Hemingway's definition of courage: "Courage is grace under pressure." May we always walk on in faith with courage in our heart. ***"Wait and hope for and expect the Lord: be brave and of good courage and let your heart be stout and enduring. Yes, wait for and hope for and expect the Lord." Psalm 27:15***

9.   What do you need courage for the most right now? Ask God to give you that grace.

_____

_____

_____

A still and confident heart...

Throughout this study I've put quite a bit of emphasis on entering the quiet place of rest as we pray. When our mind is racing and our emotions are raging, God does not seem to be speaking. As Elijah learned **in *I Kings 19:11-13*** God was not in the wind, nor the earthquake, nor the fire, but ***"After the fire (a sound of gentle stillness and) a still, small voice**. When Elijah heard the voice, he wrapped his face in his mantle and went out and stood in the entrance o the cave. And behold, there came a voice to him and said, What are you doing here, Elijah"*

Have you ever felt God say to your heart, "What are you doing? Stop trying to figure this all out. Trust Me. I've got this." I know I have, and that's why I've learned (sometimes the hard way) to ***"Let be and be still, and know (recognize and understand) that I am God. I will be exalted among the nations! I will be exalted in the earth!" Psalm 46:16*** Jesus Himself told us that His sheep hear his voice ***(John 10:27),*** so may our hearts get quiet enough to hear Him today. May we obediently respond like Samuel did when God spoke to him: ***"Speak, Lord, for Your servant is listening." I Samuel 3:10b***

In our times of intercession, as we grow to know and touch the Father's heart, <u>we will also grow in our confidence.</u> *I John 5:14-15* encourages us: *"And <u>**this is the confidence (the assurance, the privilege of boldness) which we have in Him**</u>: (we are sure) that <u>**if we ask anything (make any request) according to His will**</u> (in agreement with His own plan), <u>**He listens to and hears us,**</u> and if (since) we (positively) know that <u>**He listens to us in whatever we ask**</u> we also know (with settled and absolute knowledge) that <u>**we have (granted us as our present possessions) the requests made of Him.**</u>"*

Another wonderful promise is ***John 14:13 "And I will do (I Myself will grant) whatever you ask <u>in My Name (as presenting all that I AM)</u>, so that the Father may be glorified and extolled in (through) the Son."*** It is good to conclude our prayers saying "in Jesus' name," but as we mature, we are more and more "in Christ," in His likeness. Notice how <u>this verse adds "presenting all that I AM"</u> which to me implies we need to know the Father's heart, to really present all that He is, when we pray.

My prayer for you has already been written in ***Ephesians 3:16-21***, but here let me emphasize verses ***20-21 "Now to Him Who, by (in consequence of) the (action of His) power that is at work within us, is <u>able to (carry out His purpose and) do superabundantly, far over and above all</u> that we (dare) ask or think (infinitely beyond our highest prayers, desires, thoughts, hopes, or dreams)—<u>"To Him be glory in the church and in Christ Jesus throughout all generations forever and ever. Amen (so be it)."</u>*** So the answer to all our prayers may not be what our limited thinking expected, but <u>it may be superabundantly above all we ask or pray; and it will always be for the glory of God</u>, for it will come from His heart of love. Of that we can be most confident.

10. How have you learned to become still to hear God, and what confidence does that give you?

_____

_____

_____

_____

_____

_____

Reflecting...

In coming to the end of this study on intercession, I would like to mention again some key points. I hope you have been doing your own reflecting on your life's journey and how God has planted you in specific places for His eternal purposes. I hope you have recalled how His love has wooed you over the years to know Him better and how His grace has sustained and empowered you in tough times and in seasons of rest. My hope also is that these words, especially all the powerful scriptures, have inspired you to ponder the preciousness of your faith. And above all, I hope you've drawn closer to your own Intercessor and Advocate, Jesus, who is able to *"save to the uttermost." (Hebrews 7:25)* Never forget, *"And it shall be that before they call I will answer; and while they are yet speaking I will hear." Isaiah 65:24* Our Father is always listening to the prayers of our heart.

I believe, simply put, that our joy and responsibility as intercessors is to touch our natural circumstances (people, places and things) and to surrender them to the redeeming power of the cross. It is the Holy Spirit in us Who then is released to intercede. Sometimes we have no idea how to pray, and that's okay. That's the Holy Spirit's business, and that's why He leads us to pray in the spirit. Then that intercession touches our Advocate Jesus who brings the needs before our Father, the omnipotent God. This is how we touch the heart of God.

"But thanks be to God, Who gives us the victory (making us conquerors) through our Lord Jesus Christ. Therefore, my beloved brethren, be firm (steadfast), immovable, always abounding in the work of the Lord (always being superior, excelling, doing more than enough in the service of the Lord), knowing and being continually aware that your labor in the Lord is not futile (it is never wasted or to no purpose.)" I Corinthians 15:57-58

The foundation for our lives should be about knowing who we are in Him, accepting ourselves as He does, and trusting Him to see us through anything and everything. And the journey of our lives is about knowing Him and how much He loves us. *"And I am convinced and sure of this very thing, that He Who began a good work in you will continue until the day of Jesus Christ (right up to the time of His return) developing (that good work) and perfecting and bringing it to full completion in You. Philippians 1:6* We are to grow in our understanding and appreciation of how He works and speaks into our lives.

He needs to become our daily reality, overtaking the "reality" of natural thinking and earthly situations, as well as the lies of the strategies of the enemy which try to hinder our growth. All believers are strategically positioned to bring God's will, His Kingdom, to their corner of the world. Jesus' words in *Matthew 6:10* are a powerful intercessory prayer: *"Your kingdom come. Your will be done on earth as it is in heaven."* Yes and amen.

11. Explain how you know you are partnering with Him, to fulfill His purposes on this Earth.

_____

_____

_____

_____

_____

_____

_____